THE

Sacred

Balance

THE
Sacred
Balance

A Visual Celebration of Our Place in Nature

DAVID SUZUKI · AMANDA MCCONNELL

with Maria DeCambra

GREYSTONE BOOKS
DOUGLAS & McINTYRE PUBLISHING GROUP
VANCOUVER / TORONTO / NEW YORK

PAGE II

Dawn at Sentinel Pass, Canadian Rockies.

PAGE VI

Mussel shell.

Greystone Books
A division of Douglas & McIntyre Ltd.
2323 Quebec Street, Suite 201
Vancouver, British Columbia V5T 4S7
www.greystonebooks.com

NATIONAL LIBRARY OF CANADA CATALOGUING IN PUBLICATION DATA

Suzuki, David, 1936–
    The sacred balance: a visual celebration of our place in nature

    ISBN 1-55054-966-9

    1. Natural history—Pictorial works. 2. Human ecology.
3. Social ecology. I. McConnell, Amanda. II. DeCambra, Maria,
1970– II. Title.

GF80.S88 2002   304.2   C2002-910755-5

Library of Congress Cataloguing information is available.

Editing by Nancy Flight
Jacket and text design by Val Speidel
Front jacket photograph by Galen Rowell/Mountain Light
Back jacket photograph by James R. Page
Illustration by Stuart Daniel
Printed and bound in Canada by Friesens
Distributed in the U.S. by Publishers Group West

This book is printed on paper that is 10 per cent post-consumer waste.

The quote on page 29 is from *Collected Poems* by Philip Larkin.
© 1988, 1989 by the Estate of Philip Larkin. Reprinted by permission of Farrar, Straus & Giroux, LLC and by Faber & Faber Ltd.

The quote on page 90 is from *I Wouldn't Have Missed It: Selected Poems of Ogden Nash.* © 1949 by Ogden Nash, renewed. Reprinted by permission of Curtis Brown Ltd.

The publisher gratefully acknowledges the support of the Canada Council and of the British Columbia Ministry of Tourism, Small Business and Culture. The publisher also wishes to acknowledge the financial support of the Government of Canada through the Book Publishing Industry Development Program (BPIDP) for its publishing activities.

Every effort has been made to trace accurate ownership of copyrighted material used in this book. Errors or omissions will be corrected in subsequent editions, provided notification is sent to the publisher.

To the community of all life on Earth

that welcomes us so generously

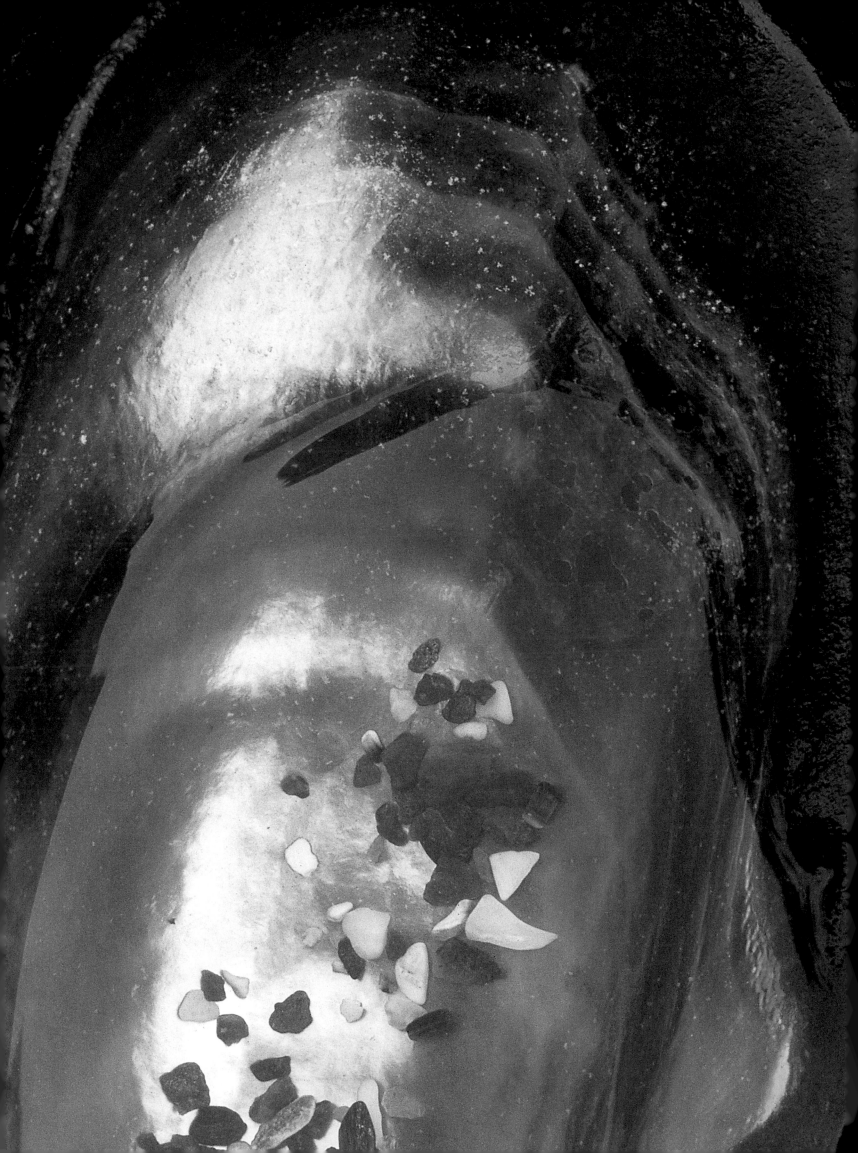

CONTENTS

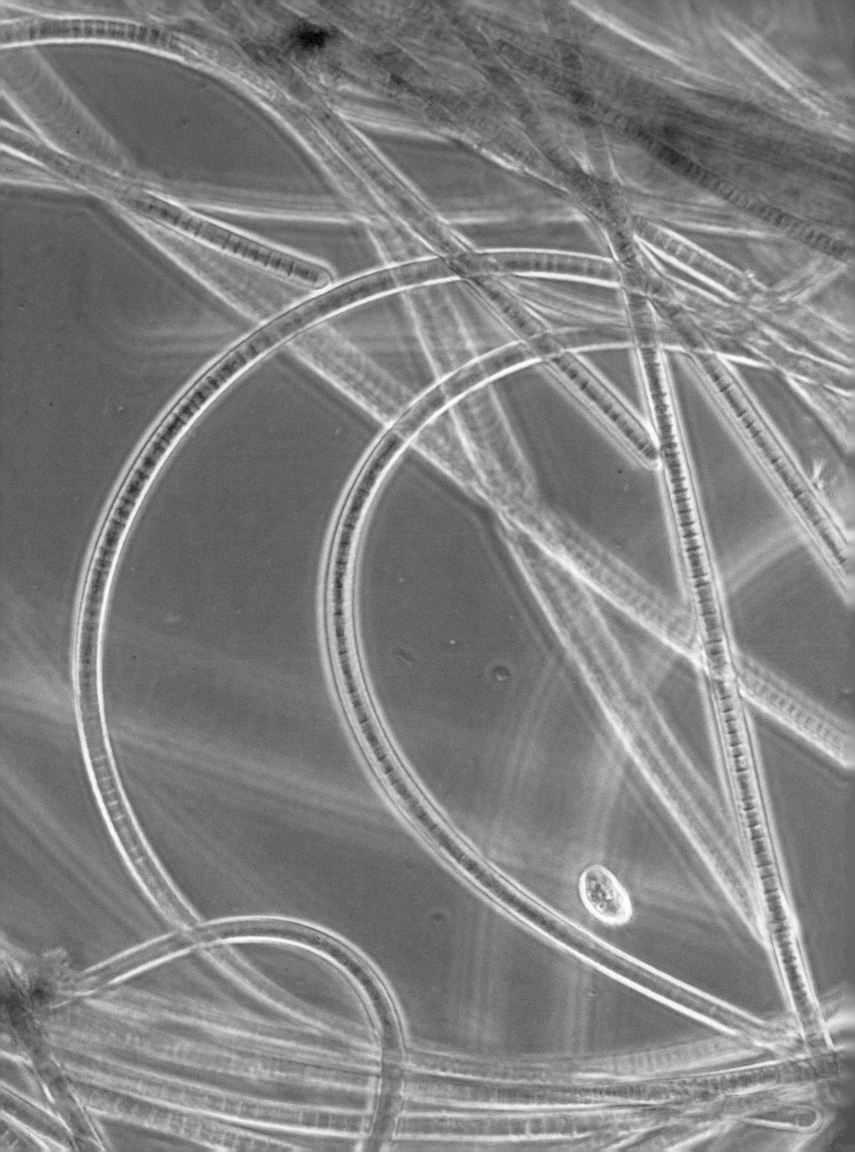

INTRODUCTION

VOLUTION endowed human beings with the most complex structure in the known universe—a brain, from which sprang curiosity, ingenuity, and imagination. With those gifts, we have looked out on a cosmos filled with mystery and enchantment and tried to make sense of it. We have pondered who we are, why we are here, and where we are going. The many varied answers to these questions have formed the underpinnings of diverse cultures that taken together make up the ethnosphere—the cosmos as created by all of human intellect, imagination, and dreaming.

Like all biological beings, we have limits. We are confined by the perceptive range of our sense organs and by the capacity of our brains to analyze the sensory signals we are able to capture. Some of our fellow creatures, having followed different evolutionary paths, may sense what we cannot. Dogs are sensitive to high-pitched sounds, for example, and moths to ultraviolet light. Other creatures fail to register what we find obvious, like fishes that are blind to certain colours.

In the past century, science and technology have expanded our limits, greatly amplifying our capacity to catalogue and process information around and within us. Armed with radio telescopes, DNA hybridization techniques, spectrophotometers, electron microscopes, magnetic resonance imaging devices, and supercomputers, we have gained insights into a universe that is far more extraordinary than we ever imagined yet exhibits a remarkable congruence with the cosmos as described by traditional bodies of knowledge. This universe is one in which everything is inextricably interconnected, and this is the awe-inspiring story that is now emerging.

A NEW WAY OF SEEING

To capture the sweep of this modern story of interconnections, imagine that somewhere in another galaxy far away there are beings who can instantly perceive, through their senses alone, the entire spectrum of information that we painstakingly piece together through both our senses and our instruments. And suppose some of these beings are scientists who travel through the cosmos in search of life elsewhere. On their journey they would observe the continuing expansion of the universe and feel the rumbles and reverberations that are the echoes of the Big Bang of the Creation thirteen billion years ago. These alien explorers would see that every component of the cosmos, from the smallest elementary particle to the largest supergalaxy, is instantly influenced by and thus "aware" of and connected through forces of attraction to every other component. The seeming emptiness of space is an illusion of our limited sensory capacity, for it

OPPOSITE PAGE

The green magic of bacteria used the power of the Sun to transform the planet.

is filled with the evanescent tendrils of yearning that every particle of matter has for all others. There is no loneliness or isolation in a universe crammed with a matrix of allurement.

Our visitors from space, having passed by hundreds of billions of the trillion galaxies in the cosmos, eventually encounter the great wheel of our Milky Way. There they behold 200 billion stars, many surrounded by moons and planets, all held together by the forces of attraction. Orchestrated by the physical rules of mass, momentum, and gravity, every one of these bodies dances and spins in elegant geometric patterns. Near the outer edge of the galactic wheel, our star, the Sun, is no more than a modest nuclear furnace among the pantheon of celestial bodies. But it is still an awe-inspiring sight. The Sun contains 99.58 per cent of all the matter in its solar system, making it a million times bigger than its third satellite, our home, planet Earth.

Drawn together by immense gravitational forces in the Sun's interior, hydrogen nuclei are pulled through the barriers of repulsion, then fused and transmogrified into helium. In the process they liberate photons of energy. The energy of each photon released is transferred to neighbouring atoms, which in turn are fused and transformed. The process continues in an erratic but unbroken chain until the energy of a photon produced at the centre of the Sun finally reaches the surface thirty thousand to forty thousand years later.

Burning 4 million tonnes of hydrogen every second, the Sun consumes itself to send forth a gift of heat and light in all directions. In eight minutes, photons leap across 150 million kilometres of space to illuminate and energize our planet. Only a narrow beam of one-billionth of all the Sun's emitted photons reaches Earth, yet that provides all the energy needed to keep the planet from plunging towards absolute zero, a temperature inimical to life.

Arriving at our solar system, those explorers from distant reaches of the cosmos would instantly perceive the presence of life on Earth. The remarkable maintenance of the planet's rich, reactive atmosphere of oxygen, methane, and water and the stability of its temperature and marine salinity both attest to the interaction of living organisms with the geophysical matrix of the planet. Unlike the living Earth, Venus and Mars, which lack life, have atmospheres that are dominated by carbon dioxide and have no reactive gases. It is through this perpetual interaction that life maintains the conditions it needs to thrive.

Life's prime requisite is abundantly on display on Earth's surface and in its atmosphere. Seventy per cent of the globe is covered with water, while ice sheets, clouds, and vapour cloak the rest of it. The space travellers would observe water molecules evaporating from oceans, rivers, and lakes, popping through the taut surface into the air. They would see the mat of vegetation on land pulling water from soil and propelling it into the air through transpiration. And they would see water vapour rising into the skies and flowing in great rivers of moisture across the continents, condensing, falling, and rising again in the hydrologic cycle that maintains the planet's life.

The observers from space would also see that water had prepared a place for life. In Earth's early days, over hundreds of millions of years, water leached atoms and minerals from rock and absorbed compounds from the atmosphere to form a chemical broth in the oceans. In that rich prebiotic soup of chemicals and molecules, life made its appearance some 3.8 billion years ago and eventually filled the planet with its descendants. For most of life's existence, it was a bacterial world.

Marine organisms absorbed carbon dioxide that was dissolved in oceans and sequestered it in the earth as limestone. In the sea cyanobacteria learned to capture sunlight through photosynthesis and, as a byproduct of the process, created oxygen, which was released into the atmosphere.

In doing so, life introduced fire to the planet. Oxygen

fashioned combustion in all its forms: from the controlled process of metabolism to the wild conflagration of fire. Photosynthesis was life's means of harnessing the Sun's beneficence: some bacteria built themselves out of sunlight, while others, incapable of photosynthesis on their own, became receptacles for those that could. Organisms with specialized functions, such as the ability to move, to respire oxygen, or to photosynthesize, invaded other bacteria to become integral parts of their hosts. This formation of symbiotic relationships, wherein one organism combines forces with another for mutual benefit, is called symbiogenesis and made multicellularity possible. All plants and animals are the product of symbiogenesis; all large organisms, including us, are the result of ancient collaborations.

The image of the self, the individual we perceive in the mirror, is deceiving. We cannot see it, but the scientists from outer space would recognize that each of us is a community of perhaps 60 trillion cells. Almost every one of those cells contains hundreds of organelles, which are descendants of ancient bacteria that invaded the cells. Cells and organelles all act in harmony to create something considerably more than the sum of their parts—a thinking, self-aware individual.

Trees, the leviathans of the plant kingdom, reach up to the sky in supplication for sunlight. They transform

We are all one. Birds, plants, animals, minerals—we are all different manifestations of the same essential energy. Our way ahead, our searches and dreams are the molecular expression of the life experience of everything that makes up our planet. By caring for it, we will help each other to grow.

—Alejandro Lerner, Argentinian writer and composer

OPPOSITE PAGE AND ABOVE

Travellers through the cosmos discover Earth. It's an island of life in the cold seas of space.

OPPOSITE PAGE

Life piles upon life everywhere on the planet, especially
in the temperate rain forest.

the Sun's gift into chemical energy that can be stored and incorporated into their being. Packed with chloroplasts that are the descendants of parasitic cyanobacteria, plants capture and store energy that then ripples through the biosphere, absorbed by other plants, animals, fungi, and microorganisms. When they die plants accumulate over vast intervals of time to become fossil fuels—coal, oil, and gas. As we grow, move, and reproduce, the energy that originated in the Sun is liberated inside us as a cascade of invisible scintillating metabolic flashes.

Like other animals, we take the bodies of other life forms into our digestive tract and leach energy and molecular building blocks from them to replenish the fuel and structure of our bodies. Animals, plants, and microorganisms are inseparably meshed, feeding and being fed upon in the intricate drama of life, death, and decay. In this world of multitudinous life forms, one species' wastes become another's nourishment, as death gives birth to new life.

On land, macromolecules created by life seep from carcasses into sand, silt, and clay to form soil, a medium for exploitation by a new menagerie of creatures. Our alien arrivals, whose senses can detect the microscopic and penetrate rock and soil, will find Earth's greatest efflorescence of life beneath its surface. As direct descendants of life's earliest forms, bacteria evolved all

of the basic genetic, metabolic, physiological, and regulatory properties on which more complex forms are based. And in the earth, microbes continue to rule; their biomass exceeds the weight of all the other living things on Earth. Able to survive at temperatures above boiling, under enormous atmospheric pressure, and in high levels of salt and acidity, bacteria extend their realm to the ocean depths and to kilometres below solid ground. Even the rocks have bacteria embedded within them and could be thought of as alive.

Standing outside the human physical perception of the temporal, our researchers from space experience the immense convulsions of Earth's history like a video on fast-forward. Over billions of years, the Sun increases its output by 30 per cent; continents glide like skateboards to collide and separate; oceans flood vast areas and then drain; rivers slice gashes into the landscape in their relentless run to the sea; glaciers spread and then dissolve into periods of warmth and lush growth. All the while life changes, adapts, and flourishes. Diversity reveals itself to be the strategy for survival—diversity of genes within each species, of species within ecosystems, and of ecosystems around the planet—for as changes occur, life's resilience depends on the pool of differences from which new gene, species, and ecosystem combinations might flourish under the altered conditions.

The visitors have arrived in time to witness the full flowering of the web of life on Earth. In the last quintile of life's existence, multicellular creatures emerged in a profusion of forms, sizes, and shapes that could swim the seas, soar into the heavens, and race across the land. Guided by external magnetic, stellar, and molecular cues and impelled by internal cycles of hormones and maturation, grey whales, Pacific salmon, sea birds, and monarch butterflies journey thousands of kilometres across the hemispheres to birthing, spawning, and feeding grounds. The oceans resonate with a cacophony of clicks, pops, high-pitched squeals, and deep reverberations of communication. On land, even in the most barren "wasteland" of desert, tundra, and scrubland, life persists and, at times, abounds. Our alien visitors would see such land crisscrossed with the paths of animals and with the traditional traplines, seasonal movement, and trails of hunting-and-gathering peoples. Evolution has filled Earth and fully developed it.

The air is laden with the inhalations and expirations of plants and animals; with molecular signals that inform, beckon, or warn companions, mates, gametes, or predators; and with a wide spectrum of vibrations that are sound, much of it inaudible to our ears but detectable by other species and our instruments. We don't end at our skin. We exude an aura of water mole-

cules, radiate a mantle of heat, and exhaust a cloud of gas. Just as a dog recreates scenes from days-old spoor, !Kung trackers read the telltale signs of passing game, and scientists interpret the echoes from the universe's birth, our spaceborne scientists would draw conclusions from the ephemeral apparition of heat, breath, and moisture left behind as we pass by.

When humans emerged along the Rift Valley of Africa, we were surrounded by our closest primate kin. The most remarkable revelation gained from deciphering the human genome has been the presence of fossilized genetic sequences that demonstrate our shared lineage with bacteria, plants, and other animals—they are our biological relatives. We are Earth beings, sharing genes with all other life forms through our common evolutionary history. Not only do we share this kinship, we appear to have a genetically encoded need to affiliate with them, a need that E. O. Wilson has called biophilia. Miraculously, the biological web of our kin cleanses, renews, and creates our most fundamental biological needs.

Our extragalactic visitors would not see any demarcation separating us from air, water, soil, and energy— we are born from Earth, created by those elements, and are constantly absorbing, retaining, and releasing them in altered states. We are made up of those sacred elements that flow through and around us in a world of interconnections and interdependencies that expose the notion of isolation, separation, and independence as an illusion created by our narrowed senses. Observing the collaboration of all living entities in Earth's biosphere, the alien scientists might conclude that this strange and beautiful planet they have reached is actually a single, integrated, self-regulating living system. There is a name for this vision of Earth: Gaia.

For tens of thousands of years, human beings have understood that reality: we emerged from, remain embedded in, and are utterly dependent on nature. We have known what those imagined visitors from other worlds might actually see—that everything is immutably connected to everything else and that therefore every act has consequences. Every human group has understood our absolute need for each other, for other forms of life, and for the sacred elements that together constitute creation. As conscious beings we have understood that our decisions entail responsibilities to honour the past, to protect the legacy of future generations, and to sustain the continuity of nature itself. And we have stored this understanding so that it will never be lost to our species. In countless cultures throughout time, our songs, prayers, and rituals have reaffirmed our responsibilities and our commitment to fulfil them.

Layer upon layer of complexity and interconnectiv-ity means that nothing exists in isolation and that everything has its place within the cosmos. This is the magnificent story emerging from the labs and minds of leading thinkers in the world today. But it is a story we find hard to hear. In the same century that we have acquired a new creation story that explains our origins, we have lost touch with the traditional knowledge in which it has its roots. Our species has undergone an explosive transformation from millennia of agrarian village life to the big city. We have suddenly become the most numerous mammal on Earth, possessed of a staggering array of technology that enables us to extract resources from any part of the globe. All humanity has become enmeshed in an economy built on the notion that endless growth is not only possible but also essential. And in the process we have lost our sense of place, our ancient understanding of our relationship with the world we depend on.

Big city life, technology, global telecommunications, and economics—these are some of the major forces that limit and distort our perceptions, sever our actions from their consequences. We are blind to the connections. Thus, few of us would recognize that driving five blocks instead of walking degrades the atmosphere or that buying a high-quality, cheap shirt made in India undermines the quality of life for the exploited poor. Today each of us

introduction

PAGES 10—11

Evolution has filled Earth and fully developed it.

LEFT

All life is close kin, sharing genes through its evolutionary history.

has access to more information than all of humanity had in the past; yet we are bereft of the real knowledge that we, our children, and generations yet to be born must have if we are to live full, rich, and satisfying lives. We have forgotten that we are biological creatures, totally dependent on the natural world; instead, we have become enthralled with our own cleverness and the illusion that the human economy is the source of all that matters.

We don't have extragalactic scientists to describe the universe we occupy. But the newest discoveries of science, the astonishing developments in instrumentation, are providing us with a new way of seeing the world we belong to. This new vision can restore our understanding of the intricate connections that tie us in to Earth's cycles. It can reveal the sacred balance of elements we are part of and remind us of the crucial need to keep them safe. But to do that, we have to recognize the limits to scientific insight lest we erroneously conclude that we have escaped the constraints of nature and can now manage our own destiny. What follows is the story of how one person arrived at that recognition, riding the rollercoaster of the past half-century along with everyone else.

introduction

A PERSONAL STORY

Nature has been my touchstone and reference throughout my life. My very earliest memories are of camping and fishing in British Columbia with my father. Today he would be called a naturalist; he was an avid fisherman, he loved the outdoors, and he was fascinated by plants. As a boy, I would accompany Dad on weekends to explore rivers, lakes, and forests along the coast. In retrospect, my father gave me the greatest gift I can imagine, a deeply engrained bond with and need for nature. Perhaps he merely encouraged and enhanced the expression of our innate biophilia. Throughout my boyhood—deep in the Rocky Mountains, in rural southern Ontario, and in the vibrant city of London, Ontario—nature filled me with wonder and enchantment.

During the postwar years, opportunity seemed limitless. The North American economy was pulled out of the depths of the Great Depression by World War II, which demanded machines of death and destruction. The American economy blazed hot as the engine of the "free world," and in the postwar era economists found a way to keep it growing—consumption. Today two-thirds of the American economy is generated by consumption. In the nineteenth century, *consumption* referred to a wasting away from tuberculosis; in the second half of the twentieth century, the word described a key to individual fulfilment and continued economic growth. It is only Earth that is wasting away from that consumption.

The consequences are reflected in London, Ontario. A hub of economic activity, the city had a population of seventy thousand and was growing rapidly when my family arrived in 1949. I spent countless hours of my youth fishing on the Thames River, and in the process, I came to know every riffle and pool in the river, the best bait for black bass, and the timing of the annual spawning runs of pike, silver bass, and walleyes. When I was free of chores and homework, I could ride my bike along a dirt road for half an hour to reach a magical place filled with mystery and surprise—a swamp. It was there that I first spotted a bittern in the reeds with its beak held straight up, trying to be invisible. I thrilled to the sight of foxes and skunks, and I would return home muddy but triumphant with salamander or frog eggs. A further twenty minutes away was my grandparents' farm, where I spent many summer days in the field or the creek watching pheasants, searching for freshwater clams, or hunting for turtles. These were among my most indelible biology lessons.

Today London is a city transformed. In merely half a century, it has grown by more than 500 per cent to exceed 400,000 people. As a consequence, the Thames River is so polluted that the suggestion that one might fish in it, let alone eat something caught from it, is met with horror. My enchanted swamp is buried beneath a massive shopping centre and parking lot. Now my grandparents' farm grows highrise apartments, while my beloved creek flows through underground tiles. So where do youngsters in London today find their inspiration? The endless variety and surprise of nature that enthralled me as a boy have been replaced by the glitter of our own creations—electronic games, shopping malls, and the virtual world of the Internet.

In the fall of 1957, I was in my fourth year at Amherst College in Massachusetts when an epidemic of Asian flu swept North America and soon claimed me as a victim. I staggered to the college infirmary and signed in as a patient. Listlessly listening to the radio, I was electrified to hear the announcement that the Soviet Union had successfully launched a satellite, Sputnik, into orbit around the Earth.

In the ensuing months, which dragged into years, the Americans attempted to duplicate the Soviet feat—only to fail spectacularly while the nation watched on television. Meanwhile, the Soviets announced one space first after another—the first animal (the dog, Laika), the first person (Yuri Gagarin), the first team, and later, the first woman (Valentina Tereshkova) to travel in space. In the agonizing aftermath of Sputnik, the Soviets seemed to be an invincible force whose impressive achievements were attracting much of the developing world into its political orbit. Belatedly we realized the Soviet Union was highly advanced in mathematics, engineering, physics, and medicine, and so the United States launched a program to catch up. NASA was established, and agencies such as NSF were beefed up to administer research and development, as billions were poured into universities and student aid.

Even though I was a Canadian attending college in the United States, I became a beneficiary of the massive infusion of funding in science. I entered the Department of Zoology of the University of Chicago to work with a specialist on the genetics of the fruitfly, *Drosophila melanogaster.* It was a golden period for a budding scientist. We came to believe in science as the purest, most powerful way of knowing: through its insights, we believed, we would push back the curtains of ignorance and reveal the deepest secrets of the cosmos. We assumed that with science we could master the world around us and that life would get better and better for all of humanity.

We graduate students were impelled by the sheer joy of pitting our intellect against the unknown. As a novice, I learned to focus on genes, chromosomes, and hereditary processes and probe them with an arsenal of genetic tools and techniques. This was "reductionism," whereby the fly was simply a vehicle for our studies. In fact, we used to refer to the fly as a "bag of chromosomes." We called ourselves "chromosome mechanics" who could tinker with the structure and arrangement of genes and chromosomes, and there was a camaraderie among the small coterie of such experts around the world. It never occurred to us that in focussing on a part of nature, we were losing sight of the context—the rhythms, patterns, relationships, cycles—that made the phenomena we were studying interesting and meaningful in the first place.

While I was a graduate student, from 1958 to 1961, molecular biology was exploding in vigour and excitement as researchers working with bacteria, viruses, or cell extracts in test tubes were elucidating the main features of how genes control cellular processes.

Drosophila geneticists began to apply some of the molecular techniques to study the protein products controlled by single genes in individual flies. It was assumed that a highly evolved species such as a fruitfly would have winnowed out deleterious or less advantageous genes over time and therefore would be relatively homogeneous in makeup. To our amazement, the opposite was found: many different genes existed in a wide array of states, a condition that has come to be known as genetic polymorphism. Today it is taken for granted that a high degree of genetic polymorphism is the very definition of

a healthy, vigorous species. Genetic polymorphism provides resilience to a species when surrounding conditions change. It is the means by which a species adapts to its environment. The reason there is concern about species such as whooping cranes or Siberian tigers, which have been reduced to a small number, is that the genetic variety is so reduced that the animals may no longer be as adaptable as they should be.

I returned to Canada in 1962 to take a position in the Department of Genetics at the University of Alberta. My work eventually led me to attempt to find a new set of genes involved in cell division. In order to recover them, I had to find genes that would express themselves under one set of environmental conditions but not under another. I chose temperature as the controlling condition, and to my delight, I found that temperature-sensitive mutations were readily induced and recovered in *Drosophila.* Temperature-sensitivity of mutations was a useful property that could be used to investigate many areas of physiology, development, and behaviour.

Later, when my interest had shifted to environmental issues, my genetic work offered relevant lessons, the most important being that an organism does not exist in isolation; it must be seen in the context of its surroundings. What I had shown was that at certain temperatures a fly carrying a temperature-sensitive mutation would appear

We need nature more than nature needs us. It should be looked on with awe and humility.

—Prince Sadruddin Aga Khan, President of the Bellerive Foundation

to be perfectly normal, while a temperature shift of a few degrees warmer or cooler could induce severe abnormalities or death. How, then, could an organism be examined without considering the ecological context within which it is reared? Furthermore, a fly's sensitivity to temperature under lab conditions warns of the hazards of global shifts in temperature for entire species and ecosystems in the wild.

In 1962, while embarking on a fresh career in genetics, I began what would turn out to be a second occupation in television. In the same year, I was profoundly influenced, as were millions of other people around the world, by Rachel Carson's seminal book, *Silent Spring.* In this book, she documented the unexpected and catastrophic consequences of chemical pesticides; her warnings about the unintended consequences of technology gave birth to the first wave of environmentalism.

Moving to British Columbia in 1963, I became involved in protests against American nuclear bomb tests in Amchitka (which were the stimulus for the formation of Greenpeace), the dam proposed at site C on the Peace River, clear-cut logging, offshore drilling for oil, and air and water pollution from pulp mills. The way I perceived the problems was that we humans were removing too much from our surroundings and putting too much toxic material back into the environment. So, in this way of thinking, the solution was to set limits on *how much* and *what* we could remove and on *how much* and *what* we could put back—and then to enforce those limits. Thus, in addition to protesting, we were lobbying politicians to pass laws—Clean Water Acts, Clean Air Acts, Endangered Species Acts— and to set up the infrastructure to enforce them.

As I became more involved in these issues from the 1960s to the '70s, however, it gradually became clear to me that such ideas about how to deal with environmental problems were misguided. They couldn't work because we didn't know enough to enable us to set limits.

Let me illustrate. DDT had been synthesized in the late 1800s, but it wasn't until the 1930s that Paul Mueller, working for Geigy in Switzerland, discovered that the compound kills insects. The economic benefits for Geigy, which trumpeted the imminent conquest of insect pests and associated diseases, were obvious. Sales of DDT rose rapidly, especially during and after World War II. Shortly after the war, when we were living on a farm, my mother would put dinner on the table and then spray DDT directly over the food; the cloud would settle onto our plates. We believed the claims that this potent pesticide killed insects but was completely harmless to people. Films from the '50s show children playing in clouds of DDT sprayed in school yards, and commercials promoted products such as paint containing DDT that would kill

introduction

insects for months. Mueller won a Nobel Prize in 1948 for his discovery.

At the time DDT sales took off, enough was known to argue for at least a judicious use of the insecticide. Geneticists already knew, for example, that resistant mutants would soon replace the insecticide-sensitive insects, making DDT far less effective, and ecologists could have pointed out that it makes little sense to use a broad-spectrum compound that kills all insects just to attack the handful that are pests to humans. But the idea that these pests might be eradicated by human ingenuity overrode any objections.

It was only after millions of kilograms of DDT had been used over years that birdwatchers began to notice that raptors such as eagles were disappearing. Tracing the cause, biologists discovered that the birds' eggshells were thinning. This discovery led scientists to the hitherto unknown phenomenon of biomagnification. In this process the concentration of a substance in an organism increases as the molecule moves up the food chain, so that it might be quite low in a microorganism but much higher in a bird or mammal. At each trophic level up the food chain, DDT is concentrated severalfold until in the fatty tissue of shell glands of birds (and breasts of women), DDT is found at hundreds of thousands of times the original concentration. Because biologists had

not known about biomagnification, there was no way that safe levels of DDT could have been established when the molecule first began to be used as an insecticide.

The history of chlorofluorocarbons (CFCs) demonstrates a similar absence of scientific knowledge. Like DDT, CFCs were first hailed as miracles of chemistry. These complex molecules are chemically inert and therefore make ideal nonreacting additives for filling spray cans along with compounds such as deodorants. Only after millions of kilograms of CFCs were synthesized and released did scientists find that because they are stable, they persist in the environment and eventually float into the upper atmosphere. There ultraviolet rays from the sun strike CFCs and knock off chlorine free radicals, which are potent reactants with ozone. No one could have anticipated the effects of CFCs on the ozone layer, and therefore restricted their use, because ozone depletion was only discovered as a result of the widespread use of CFCs.

There is no reason to doubt that genetically modified organisms (GMOs) will also have unexpected effects. Our ability to transfer genes between unrelated species is unprecedented. But the principles of heredity have been derived by breeding males and females of the same species, following their offspring, and breeding them. When pieces of DNA are transferred between species, we can no longer assume that the same principles of inheritance

A deep sense of connection with the planet persists in indigenous
communities around the world. I first encountered this view of
the world on Haida Gwaii, the home of the Haida, off Canada's
west coast.

introduction

apply. After all, following fertilization, genes are turned on and off in precise temporal sequence to produce a fully differentiated and developed individual. Natural selection does not act on each gene individually but on the expression of the entire genome through development. When a piece of DNA from an unrelated species is transferred into a cell, the genome and the cellular context within which it finds itself is completely new. This situation is comparable to pulling Bono out of U2, popping him into the middle of the New York Philharmonic Orchestra, and asking him to "do his thing" with them. Sounds will emerge, but we certainly cannot anticipate the musical nature of the output.

Back in the 1960s and 1970s, I was an exuberant researcher caught up in the excitement and exhilaration of experimentation and discovery. I believed that science was the most profound way of knowing and would ultimately benefit all of humankind. But my growing involvement in environmental issues as an activist and journalist forced me to confront the severe constraints of the very reductionism I had practised as a scientist. By the late 1970s, I was also well aware of the global scale of ecological problems that were being created by human activity. Towards the end of that decade, I learned about a battle between forest companies, environmentalists, and Haida people over logging in Haida Gwaii (Queen

Charlotte Islands). After years of confrontation and protests, the Haida and environmentalists had decided to draw the line at Windy Bay, an exquisite 3040-hectare watershed of old-growth forest that the forest company intended to clear-cut.

I flew up to interview forest company officials, loggers, environmentalists, Haida, and politicians. One of the interviewees was a young Haida carver and artist named Guujaaw, who had led the opposition to logging for years. I knew that the Haida had high unemployment and that logging provided many of them with jobs. Furthermore, the employees of the forest company patronized Haida stores and restaurants, so they contributed to the economy of the community. Yet Guujaaw told me, "Our people have determined that Windy Bay and other areas must be left in their natural condition so that we can keep our identity and pass it on to following generations. The forests, those oceans are what keep us as Haida people today."

"So, if they're logged off?" I asked him.

He replied, "If they're logged off, we'll probably end up the same as everyone else, I guess."

At the time, I didn't fully appreciate what he meant, but later, on reflection, I realized that he had opened a window on a radically different way of seeing the world. He was telling me that the Haida do not believe they end at their fingertips or skin. Being Haida means being connected to the land, a land that embodies their history, their culture, and the very explanation of why they are on this earth. The trees, fish, birds, and rivers of Haida Gwaii are all what make the Haida who they are.

Since then I have travelled to many parts of the world, meeting indigenous people in Borneo, the Kalahari, the Amazon rain forest, the Arctic, Japan, and Australia. And everywhere the sense of connection with the land is the same. Even in the most oppressed, impoverished, dysfunctional communities, there persists a sense of connection with Earth that is fundamentally different from the dominant culture's view.

Nonaboriginal people can have such an understanding of their attachment to a place on Earth too. I recognize it when a fourth-generation Saskatchewan farmer refuses to turn over his land to the bank because he intends to pass it on to his children and grandchildren; it is there in the people of the isolated outports of Newfoundland who refused to leave what was their home in exchange for running water and electricity in the cities. I saw it in the brilliant young Australian scientist who declined a professorship at Harvard because he wanted to go home, where he could make a contribution to his own country. These decisions mirror the aboriginal sense of where we belong on Earth.

As I reflected on these lessons, I realized that we have framed the problem improperly—there is no environment "out there" that is separate from us. Aboriginal people are right; we *are* the Earth, created like everything else from the four sacred elements of water, air, fire, and earth. This statement isn't meant in a metaphoric or poetic way but as scientifically demonstrable reality. When we think of the "environmental crisis" this way, our response has to be completely different.

We are water in the most obvious way. More than half the weight of every human being on Earth is water. A glass of water contains countless molecules circulated around the planet by the water cycle. Water is the glue that holds life together. But how can we boast of intelligence and foresight when we deliberately release toxic materials into water and therefore inject it into ourselves?

We are also air. If the planet were reduced to the size of a basketball, the atmosphere would be thinner than a sheet of plastic wrap. And that air is not constantly recreated afresh; it moves through the planet's living organisms, giving life and receiving their emissions. Increasingly, the exhalations of our machines have been added to that thin layer and are mounting up. We must breathe every minute of our lives. There is no boundary

introduction

The Earth is giving us so much. We should listen to the Earth and its heartbeat,

and live in harmony with this beautiful planet.

—Yoko Ono, *Earth Piece* (Summer 1990)

between air and ourselves because we are fused to air and it is always in us. The air we breathe out goes into the bodies of those next to us. Air is not an empty space or vacuum; it's a physical substance that binds us together and links us with trees and birds and worms and snakes that share that air. We boast of our great intelligence, but, again, what intelligent creature, knowing the life-giving role air plays for all organisms, would deliberately release the most toxic compounds into that air? Whatever we do to the air, we do to ourselves.

We are fire because energy makes all life possible, and every bit of that energy was once sunlight. All the energy we need to move, grow, and reproduce came from the Sun through photosynthesis. But we take far more than our fair share of the Sun's gift to Earth, and our profligate use of fossil fuels, the planet's stored solar energy, is imperilling our own future.

We are earth because every bit of the nutrition that we consume to create our bodies and minds was once living and almost all of it came from the soil. Basically, we are compost heaps for the carcasses of plants and animals that we consume for our nourishment. We take other life forms into our mouths, ingest them, and incorporate their molecules into our own cells. Why, then, do we knowingly use soil for dumping our toxic effluents, as if they won't affect us?

These sacred elements—water, air, sunlight, and soil—are basic to us as biological beings. They ought to be treasured beyond price, celebrated and cherished, and fiercely protected at all costs.

The ultimate miracle is the diverse web of life itself, which creates, cleanses, and renews those four sacred elements. We are all kin, related through our evolutionary history, and in the greatest act of generosity, we create for each other the elements we need to flourish.

Water is filtered and purified by the roots of trees and other plants, soil fungi, and microorganisms. Without life, water would be loaded with heavy metals and other toxic materials leaching from the rock.

It was only after microorganisms began photosynthesis, extracting carbon dioxide from the atmosphere and releasing oxygen, that the air was transformed into the oxygen-rich medium it is today. Ever since then the green plants of the oceans and land have been managing the balance of gases in our atmosphere.

Similarly, wood, peat, oil, coal, and gas are all created by plants by means of sunlight—there was no fuel on the planet before life. Without photosynthesis there would be no oxygen in the air to enable combustion. So there would be no spark to light our lonely darkness, no flame for us to huddle around.

Before life there was no soil. Soil is created by the

OPPOSITE PAGE

Every living thing, including this fern frond, is made from the
same stuff: earth and air, fire and water.

addition of matter from decaying plants and animals to
a matrix of sand, silt, and clay. To this day, life continues
to create the soil it needs to grow in, the soil in which we
grow our food.

Diverse life forms play a central role in maintaining
the planet as a habitable place. We have no idea how this
web of life maintains and propagates itself, yet we tear at
the many communities that make it up without regard to
the consequences.

Just as we need other life forms, and just as an individual ant is not fully an ant until it exists within a
colony, so to be fully human, to lead a rich, full life, we
need others of our kind. Scientific studies reveal the central role of love in fulfilling that need. From the moment
of conception and beyond birth, child and mother function as a single unit. In the act of suckling, a baby sets
off a cascade of hormones that flood the mother's body;
a reciprocal response is triggered as signals flow through
the baby. As a child develops, social relationships affect
his or her potential. Stable, supportive families and surrounding communities are necessary for love to flourish.
Hunger and poverty, chronic unemployment, injustice,
insecurity, inequality, violence, oppression, and war all
disrupt the flow of love and create more urgent priori-
ties of immediate survival. Studies reveal the deleterious
consequences of these conditions on the physical and

psychic well-being of people. So working for full
employment, equity, justice, security, and freedom from
violence, oppression, and war is crucial to nurturing love
and the full flowering of our humanity.

Even when we have satisfied our biological and
social needs, we have another level of need that must be
fulfilled to avoid a life without focus. We are uniquely
spiritual beings with a need for spirit as profound as our
need for air, water, energy, and food. The terrible burden
imposed by our self-awareness is the knowledge of our
own mortality. Death pervades our consciousness and
fills our lives with sadness. What has helped to relieve
that load is the knowledge that although each of us will
die, nature, the very source of our existence that gave
birth to us and sustains us, will persist.

The eminent psychiatrist Stephen Jay Lifton once
told me a moving story that illustrates this point. After
the atomic bomb was dropped over Hiroshima, taking a
horrific toll in death and suffering, a rumour swept the
city. The rumour was that nothing would ever grow in
Hiroshima again. A wave of horror and despair rushed
through the survivors. Even more terrible than the tens
of thousands killed and the agony of the radiation-
exposed survivors was the notion that nature itself had
been mortally wounded. Only when grass was seen growing again did the despair subside.

introduction

introduction

introduction

The title of Bill McKibben's powerful book *The End
of Nature* expressed a thought that critics felt was too hor-
rifying to contemplate. In the most profound way, we
know that we are part of nature—that our relationship
with the natural world around us tells us who we are,
where we belong. When my father was dying at the age
of eighty-five, he was lucid, free of pain, and without
fear. He found great comfort in his belief that after his
death, when his ashes would be thrown to the winds, he
would be reborn in the forests and the eagles and the
salmon. "Every time you hear the wind sigh in the trees,
every echo of an eagle's call, each silvery flash of a coho
salmon will inform you that I am still here," he told me.

My father's deeply held belief was immediate and
personal. But it was also part of the oldest traditions of
human culture that we know. In burial caves from hundreds of thousands of years ago, in paleolithic paintings,
in stone carvings and sacred stories, in ceremonies that
bless the harvest and celebrate the hunt, human beings
have always acknowledged and celebrated their place in
the fertile unfolding cycles of life on Earth. Consciousness has enabled us to recognize that the world is alive
and that we are part of it: this ancient vision is now illu-
minated and extended by the discoveries of modern science. If we can grasp that we *are* the world we depend on,
then we will find where we truly belong and get on with
seeking a way to live in harmony within a rich, vibrant
community of living things.

WATER

The Ocean Flowing Through Our Veins

If I were called in
To construct a religion . . .
I should raise in the east
A glass of water
Where any-angled light
Would congregate endlessly.

—Philip Larkin, "Water"

PAGE 28

Dewdrops glisten on a spider's web.

OPPOSITE PAGE

Vapour, liquid, solid. Water's metamorphoses coexist in this Arctic landscape.

BELOW, TOP

In its endless shimmering dance the water molecule shifts partners up to 100 billion times a second.

BELOW, BOTTOM

The microscopic tartigrade, or "water bear," can lie desiccated and dormant for a century, waiting for a single drop of water to revive it.

O UR planet flaunts its most precious possession, wrapping itself in gauzy veils that drift over a moving, glinting surface. Below the clouds, perched on dry land, we humans may forget our personal connection with the world's first wonder. We believe ourselves to be solid flesh, but like every other living thing on Earth, we are made of water. From the raindrop to the mighty ocean, water shapes the world we know.

The metamorphoses of water keep the world alive at every level, from the planetary to the cellular. Ninety-nine per cent of all chemistry on Earth takes place in water. Inside and beyond the cell wall, water is the medium or the catalyst for most of the critical exchanges of the biological world. Water's starring role can be expressed in two astonishing absolutes: as far as we know, no life has ever evolved to exist without water, and wherever there is water there is the possibility of life.

Water is our familiar companion through the days of our life. We boil it and stir it, breathe it out and in, drink it and wash ourselves in it. We know water intimately. But to chemists and physicists, it is a mysterious, intriguing anomaly. Its molecular structure gives it unique properties that play out around the planet. Two small atoms of hydrogen are attached asymmetrically to one large bulging atom of oxygen. Because the oxygen

atom has a negative charge and the hydrogen atoms have a positive charge, these little boomerang shapes are dipolar: they act like tiny magnets, attracting other water molecules tens, even hundreds, of molecules away. Clinging together, breaking apart, they shift partners with breakneck speed, creating a liquid that hangs together with high internal cohesion. This powerful affinity is called the hydrogen bond: an embrace so powerful it holds the world together.

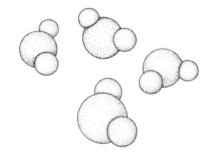

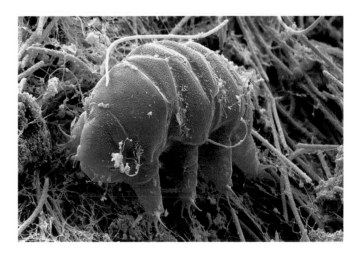

And with water we have made all living things. —The Koran, Sura XXI (Al Anbiya):30

OPPOSITE PAGE

Water's movement around the planet keeps Earth fit for life.

Water holds together so strongly that it takes a great deal to break its molecules apart; it absorbs quantities of heat before it melts, boils, or vaporizes. Water's ability to store heat works to moderate Earth's climate, as ocean currents move from the tropics to the poles. The Gulf Stream brings gifts of warmth and liveability north to Canada's east coast, where it meets and mingles with the Arctic waters of the Labrador Current before moving across the ocean to wrap the British Isles. In winter in Antarctica, as seawater freezes into ice, salt is extruded and concentrated so that water becomes supercooled and superdense, sinks to the bottom, and flows in immense, slow-moving "rivers" carrying ice-cold water around the Indian Ocean, past the tip of Africa, and northward deep in the Pacific trench. In the atmosphere water eases seasonal transitions, and in the cell it is part of the organism's ability to adapt to temperature change.

Eventually even water must relinquish its hold on heat, and when its molecules finally freeze they form a lattice that has larger spaces than exist in the liquid form. This structure enables ice to float. Just imagine what would happen in the lakes and rivers of Earth's colder regions if ice sank. What aquatic life would survive?

Liquid, vapour, ice: these transformations keep the world alive. Each year thousands of billions of cubic metres of water drop from the skies; most of it is evaporated back into the atmosphere, only to fall and rise again. Cartwheeling round the planet, water moves endlessly through the hydrologic cycle, distilled from the salt oceans into fresh water as it evaporates, condenses, and precipitates, fostering growth as it runs off into lakes and rivers and eventually drains back into the oceans. Life forms play an active part in maintaining this cycle that is so crucial to their survival: organisms absorb, filter, and transpire water back into the atmosphere.

Like each of us individually, all life was first born from water. Current scientific thinking locates the birthplace and nursery of life at the bottom of the ocean or in the wet fissures of deep rock. Close to 4 billion years ago, using energy from the centre of Earth, the mobile molecules of water helped to link free-floating atoms together, forming the complex chemical compounds that were the basis for life. Much, much later, when life forms emerged from the water onto land, they carried the water they needed with them, tucked safely behind the cellular wall.

We are three-quarters water when we are born, desiccating down to about 50 per cent as we age. Every day we need to replace about 3 per cent of our body water lost to breath, sweat, urine, feces. We live on land, but we exist in water, our own hydrologic cycle moving continually through us. The salt oceans flow in our veins. Water

molecules transpired from prairie wheatfields, evaporated from the Indian Ocean, blown in from cloud forests of Central America become part of us. Taken from the planet's store, they pass through all of us and eventually return to that store.

Throughout our species' existence on Earth we have held water to be sacred, believing it is the elixir of life. In our holiest ceremonies, water has played a central part: in the rituals of hospitality and friendship and of planting and harvest, in the welcome for a new human being, in the farewell to a departing one. But the relationship has always been uneasy: our absolute dependence confers an awe-inspiring power. Water can take away, wash away, sweep away as well as give. Today, moving ahead with our overwhelming sense of industrial and technological mastery, we are intervening everywhere in the mysterious dance of the water molecule. And we are discovering just how much we do not understand.

Central to our holiest ceremonies, water is the elixir of life. This dragon is part of a temple in Japan.

water

water

All the rivers run into the sea,

yet the sea is not full.

—Ecclesiastes 1:7

Getting water to the crop has been one of the lasting challenges to human ingenuity since we first made use of the soil. This ancient irrigation technique comes from Khajuraho in India.

Next day we were sailing in slack winds through an
ocean where the clear water on the surface was full of
drifting black lumps of asphalt, seemingly never-
ending . . . The Atlantic was no longer blue but
grey-green and opaque, covered with clots of oil ranging
from pin-head size to the dimensions of the average
sandwich. Plastic bottles floated among the waste.
We might have been in a squalid city port . . .
It became clear to all of us that mankind really was in
the process of polluting its most vital well-spring, our
planet's indispensable filtration plant, the ocean.

—Thor Heyerdahl, *The Ra Expeditions*

PAGES 38–39

The hunter at the edge of the ice is part of the spring migration,
when life converges on the rich waters of the Arctic Ocean.

OPPOSITE PAGE

In Inuit tradition Sedna rules over the kingdom of the sea.
Sometimes shown as a mermaid, sometimes as a seal, always as the
vital creative power of the cold ocean, she punishes a greedy
hunter by withholding her creatures.

w a t e r

Where Alph, the sacred river, ran

Through caverns measureless to man

Down to a sunless sea.

—Samuel Taylor Coleridge, *Kubla Khan*

OPPOSITE PAGE

One of the wondrous forms of water in an ice cave.

ABOVE

Blue sprat schooling in shallow waters.

Kaiapo women bathe in the Riozinho (Little River) in the
Brazilian state of Para.

AIR

The Breath of All Green Things

Oh there is blessing in this gentle breeze,

A visitant that while it fans my cheek

Doth seem half-conscious of the joy it brings

From the green fields, and from yon azure sky.

—William Wordsworth, "The Prelude"

a i r

PAGE 46

We can only see the air by what it carries—in this case a towering mountain of water.

OPPOSITE PAGE

Hurricane Fran, September 4, 1996. Great forces perturb the atmosphere that encloses us.

WE are made of water, yet we live in air and air lives in us: the atmosphere is the element we swim through from the moment of birth. Born out of water, catapulted into air, a new infant transforms herself to survive. Mouth opened wide, she begins a lifelong relationship with air as she takes the first of about 350 million breaths in a life span of three score and ten years. This first great gulp draws the atmosphere into the centre of the baby's being, into the labyrinthine membrane in her chest. Immediately the lungs inflate, never again to deflate fully until the long exhalation of the last breath of life. We are the air we breathe from thirteen to eighty times a minute every minute of our lives.

Oxygen is the atmospheric gas we air breathers are designed to capture, transport, and combust within our cells. Crossing the membranes deep in the lungs, its molecules attach to hemoglobin in the blood and travel throughout the body in less than a minute. Oxygen respiration lights our metabolic fires, breaking down carbohydrates and fats and releasing the energy we use for all the activities of life.

Each of us is born into a closed system, a planetary womb: the gaseous layer of Earth. It reaches 2000 kilometres into space, but almost all of it is concentrated within 30 kilometres of the planet's surface—5 million billion tonnes of air pressing down ever more densely as it approaches the ground. We are adapted to its implacable pressure: without one kilogram per square centimetre holding us together, we would explode. Creatures of the air, we are held in an atmospheric matrix that passes through us as we steal its oxygen.

Life has a right to that oxygen, however—it was life that put it there in the first place and maintains its level to this day. This process of releasing oxygen was a great turning point in the planet's history. More than 3 billion years ago, an organism related to the modern cyanobacteria started a revolutionary process of making food. Using the sun's energy, it split molecules of water apart, adding its hydrogen atoms to carbon dioxide from the atmosphere to make sugar, and dumping the oxygen atoms as waste into the air. The strategy was astonishingly successful, and these ancestral photosynthesizers spread across the Earth, filling the carbon-rich atmosphere with free oxygen. Oxygen was toxic to most life; other bacteria had to adapt, developing ways to absorb and finally to use the highly reactive new gas. Over millions of years, the concentration of oxygen in the atmosphere stabilized at about 21 per cent, and remains close to that level to this day.

Two elements are constantly in play: carbon, the building block of living organisms, put together by the

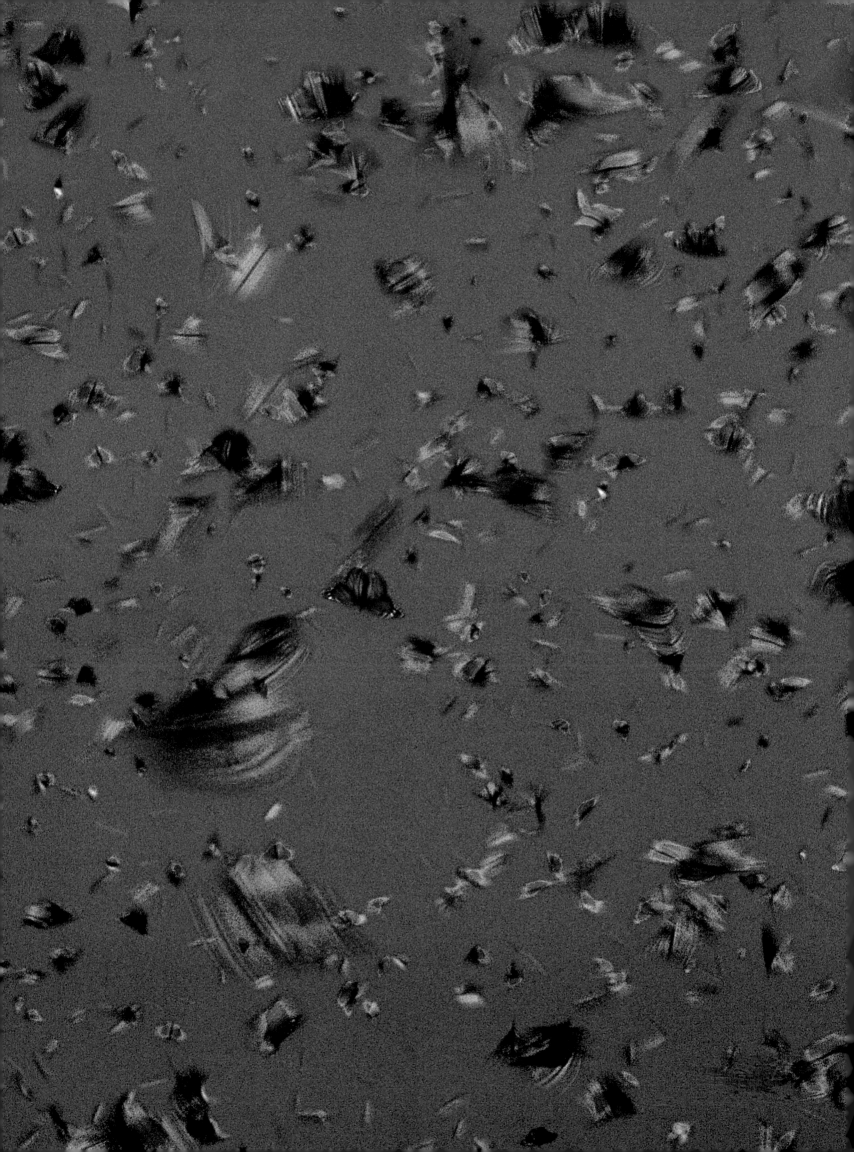

a i r

OPPOSITE PAGE

Like these monarch butterflies, we are creatures of the air, moving
in the atmosphere that moves through us.

. . . this most excellent canopy, the air, look you,

this brave o'erhanging firmament, this majestical roof

fretted with golden fire . . .

—William Shakespeare, *Hamlet*, II, 2, 298–301

sun's energy; and oxygen, the spark that breaks down the
building blocks, releasing energy. They are part of a mysterious balancing act, a reciprocal relationship between
air and the living world it sustains. It is a crucial balance:
if oxygen levels rose much higher, the world would burst
into flames; much lower, and most air breathers would
asphyxiate.

Oxygen respiration changed the world: it powered a
massive expansion and diversification of life across the
planet's surface. At the same time, the newly oxygenated
atmosphere provided land-based life with a shield against
the sun's damaging ultraviolet radiation. When ultraviolet light hits oxygen, it breaks the molecule apart and
recombines the atoms into ozone—creating the protec-
tive ozone layer.

The air that wraps Earth is a single entity, the matrix
that holds us all. It is a global commons from which we
draw the crucial element of life, sharing as we do molecules that have been breathed in and out of every living
thing that has ever breathed on Earth. Molecules that pass
through us have passed through brontosaurs, neolithic
hunters, Roman emperors, hummingbirds, snails. And
what we put into it goes up all our noses.

No part of the world is safe from the burden carried
by air. Scientists sampling the face of glaciers high in the
Rocky Mountains find a record of what the wind carried
a century ago, last year, and yesterday morning. Using
weather records, they can track the substances to their
source. Pesticides banned in Canada still fall on the pure
snow of its mountaintops; used the other side of the
world, they move through the atmosphere and condense
in the coldest, cleanest places. Radioactive isotopes
from nuclear tests fifty years ago, DDT used on prairie
fields thirty years ago, mercury, spores, pollen, clay from
eroded fields—all are preserved in the annual layers
of the Athabasca Glacier, deposited there by the all-
enfolding air.

Air is language, spirit, life. Imagine the planet's airy
creatures: the birds and gnats and butterflies, dancing in
the sun; the pollen and particles, the drift of windborne
seed, the gusting storm, the dust flung high behind the
tractor. Imagine ourselves as another creature of the
air—not drifting on the wind, but part of the atmosphere's journey through space and time. And imagine
that we treat the atmosphere as it should be treated—as
the sacred source.

Wild air, world-mothering air,

Nestling me everywhere,

.   .   .

In every least thing's life;

This needful, never spent,

And nursing element;

My more than meat and drink,

My meal at every wink;

This air, which, by life's law,

My lung must draw and draw

—Gerard Manley Hopkins, "The Blessed Virgin
compared to the Air we Breathe"

Earth and air are entwined in an invisible relationship.

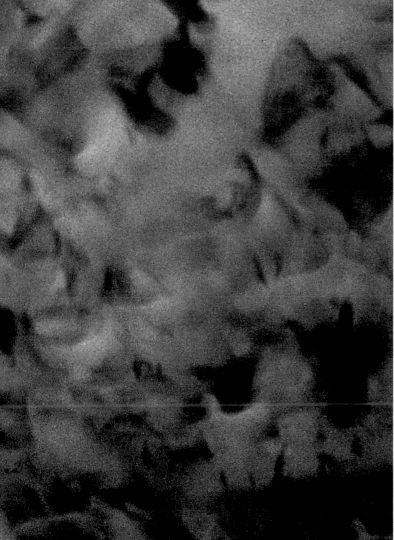

The winged kingdom has always fascinated human beings as a vision of freedom. Jan Bruegel's *Allegory of Air* was painted in 1607 for Cardinal Borromeo of Milan.

When we look into the sky it seems to us to be endless . . .

We think without consideration about the boundless ocean of air, and then you sit aboard a spacecraft,

you tear away from Earth, and within ten minutes you have been carried straight through the layer of air,

and beyond there is nothing! Beyond the air there is only emptiness, coldness, darkness.

The "boundless" blue sky, the ocean which gives us breath and protects us from the endless black and death,

is but an infinitesimally thin film. How dangerous it is to threaten even

the smallest part of this gossamer covering, this conserver of life.

—Soviet explorer Vladimir Shatalov

OPPOSITE PAGE

Who has seen the wind? All of us, shaping the world around us.

PAGES 58–59

Air at the top of the world: clouds, trees, prayer flags at
Thangboche Monastery.

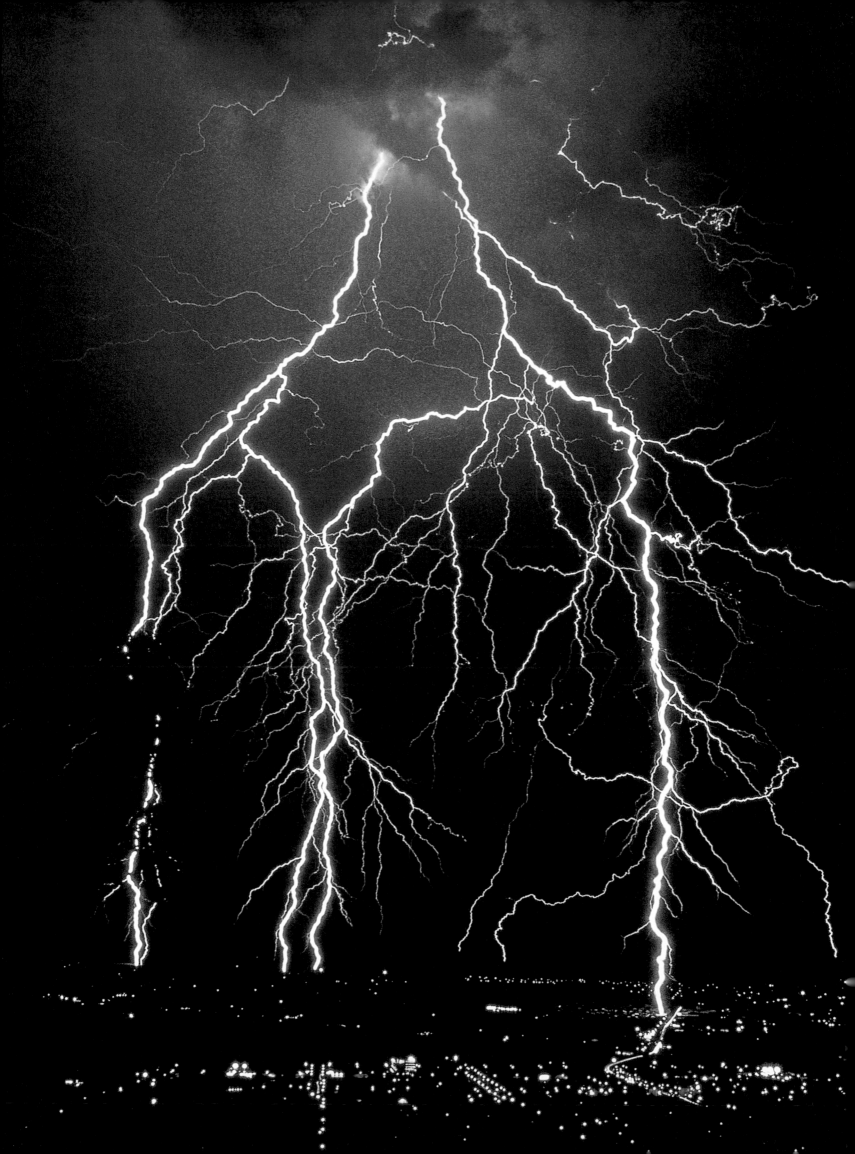

FIRE

Let There Be Light

Dazzling and tremendous how quick the sun-rise would kill me,

If I could not now and always send sun-rise out of me.

We also ascend dazzling and tremendous as the sun,

We found our own O my soul in the calm and cool of the daybreak.

—Walt Whitman, "Song of Myself"

f i r e

PAGE 60

A pulse of energy thrown by the fire god at the town of Tamworth, New South Wales.

OPPOSITE PAGE

Powered by the particles from the Sun, the aurora flames in the night sky.

FIRE is the energy of creation, the power that assembles and disassembles matter, organizing life, death, and rebirth throughout Earth. Every morning the power that drives the planet rises over its horizon. It is just one small star in a cosmos that contains billions, and we get just a tiny sliver of its radiation. But it is enough to run a planet.

Human beings have a long history of Sun worship. Who can tell how long the Plains Indians have danced their Sun dance, or what powers Inti, the Inca sun god, brought his people? Ra, the Egyptian sun god, governed all creation from his palace at Heliopolis. The Hopi start their Kachina dances in December, enticing the Sun to their desert mesas. Staying on good terms with the Sun is what really counts here on Earth. It is the most powerful object we humans can imagine—simply looking at it blinds us.

In the heart of the Sun, the temperature is 15 million degrees above absolute zero. Every second this cosmic blast furnace burns 4 million tonnes of hydrogen, releasing energy that is equivalent to 1 million 10-megatonne hydrogen bombs. It takes millennia for that photon energy to reach the surface of the Sun, where giant flares leap thousands of kilometres into space. From the Sun's surface, it takes a mere eight minutes for the stream of life-giving photons to reach the surface of the Earth, 150 million kilometres away.

Cosmologist Brian Swimme speculates about the earliest times in the cosmos and the birth of our generous Sun. He describes a long period of expansion after the big bang, and then a moment when suddenly all the stars coalesced; that was the moment when the universe came alight—and the moment it became alive. "Let there be light" was the first and only command of creation.

A living net is spread on Earth to catch the Sun. At dawn life winds up and starts to tick. Birds and mammals wake to the new day. Reptiles stretch themselves in the Sun, absorbing the heat they need to function all day. Flowers turn to the light; insects come to the flowers for nectar. The sunlit world comes alive at the microscopic level—threadworms stalking the forest of moss, dragonflies whirling at the stream's edge, spiders sitting at the centre of their webs. Trees and plants begin photosynthesis: they start to eat the sunlight. In this way, the Sun's energy cascades through the biosphere. When primitive plants evolved, about 2.5 billion years ago, with their capacity to use sunlight to make food, life on Earth began to diversify, finding many ways to access those precious energy stores. Organisms ate the plants that ate the Sun and then were eaten in their turn. This is the

f i r e

f i r e

If the eye were not sun-like,

how could it ever spy the sun?

If God's own power lay not inside us,

how could divinity delight us?

—Johann Wolfgang von Goethe, *Gedichte I 367*

On the day of the vernal equinox, dancers in tribal dress perform
in front of the Pyramid of the Sun (Teotihuacán).

energy web—the elegant, highly organized system that captures and distributes the generosity of the giant fusion engine in the sky. It includes everything alive.

Inside a leaf, chloroplast factories capture sunlight and store it in carbohydrate. Two thousand chloroplasts piled up are thinner than a dime, yet each bristles with thousands of clusters of light-trapping pigment molecules.

The chains of carbon atoms created in the chloroplasts with the Sun's energy are life's signature—they are what all life forms are made from. And they fuel life's productivity, putting the Sun to work deep inside our cells.

The planet's entire biomass is built out of carbon and hydrogen and sunlight. Food is fuel for life: it is the way we access solar energy. Our metabolism burns the products of photosynthesis to break the molecules apart, releasing the stored sunlight and putting it to work.

The same process of making and breaking is at work around us everywhere. What solar fire has put together, combustion takes apart again. In the forest, fire takes apart the carbon chains, returning the chemistry of life to the soil for use in the next cycle of growth. Fire and the natural world have had a long partnership. Life creates the fuel and the oxygen for ignition, while fire creates the conditions for new life in an endless cycle of renewal.

The planet stores energy from the Sun too, building up large deposits of organic material created by photosynthesis. Dead organisms, decayed and compressed, are transformed over hundreds of millions of years into coal, oil, and gas reservoirs of accumulated energy. This process has kept carbon out of circulation, helping to balance the gases in the atmosphere. When humans learned how to make fire, we began to alter our place in the energy web. We gathered around the fireside, shaped a culture from the sacred flame, bending it to our purposes: first to heat and cook, then to clear land and hunt our food. In many places we have completely altered the world around us with fire.

In the past we have known that fire is a two-edged sword; like all sacred things, it is both precious and dangerous. But with the invention of technology—the internal combustion engine, even the match—fire became everyone's plaything. Now our energy use in the industrialized world is altering the entire planet.

Human beings corner 40 per cent of the net output of the Sun captured by plants. After thousands of years of playing our part in the energy web, consuming energy stored over days, months, or a few years, we are now burning hundreds of millions of years of accumulated fuel. We're eating too much of the Sun, and the consequences are apparent, in cities and garbage dumps, in the air and water, in the forests and oceans of the planet. All that carbon, taken out of the atmosphere eons ago, is

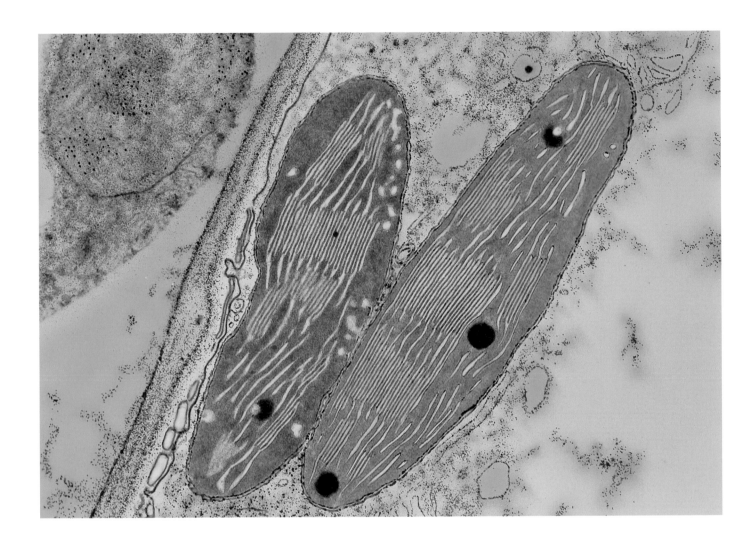

Chloroplasts are bundles of chlorophyll in leaves that capture
sunlight and create food for the plant. They evolved from
cyanobacteria, the organisms that first created Earth's
oxygenated atmosphere. Now they carry on photosynthesis
in every green plant.

f i r e

now being thrust back where it came from in an instant. An atmosphere rich in carbon dioxide traps more of the Sun's energy on Earth, but it traps it as heat, in a form we can't use, and it traps us in the turmoil of rapid climate change.

We're standing on the brink of change. All life—sunflower, rain forest, bullfrog, human being—lives by gathering up the Sun's power. But as fire historian Stephen Pyne writes, we have a species monopoly on combustion. We're the keepers of the sacred flame. Let us hope we can learn to keep it wisely.

In the arid eucalyptus bush of Western Australia, fire is the chief way life's raw materials are recycled.

fire

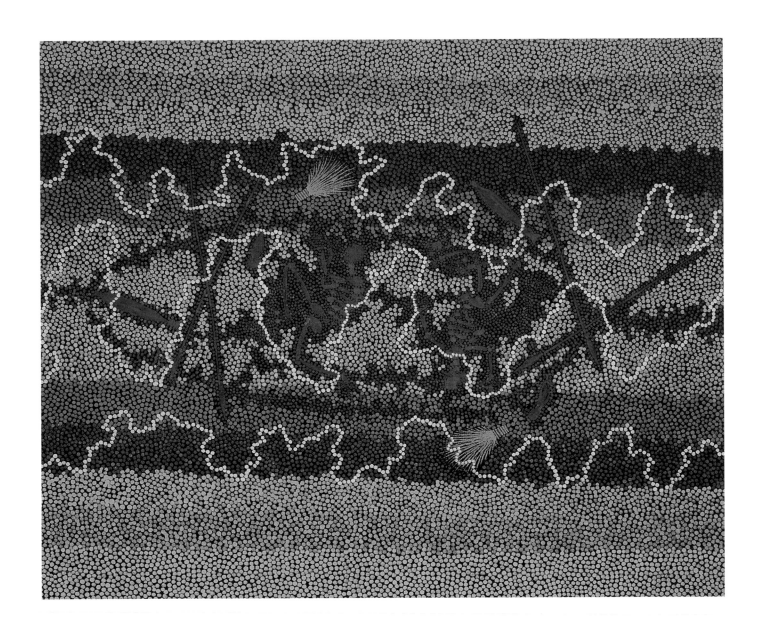

OPPOSITE PAGE

After the fire life is renewed. These are the flowerheads of the Black Gins, or Drumsticks (*Kingias*), near Mondurup Peak in Australia.

ABOVE

This Aboriginal painting is called *Bushfire Dreaming*.

Prayer for the Great Family

Gratitude to Mother Earth, sailing through night and day—
    and to her soil: rich, rare, and sweet
        in our minds so be it.

Gratitude to Plants, the sun-facing light-changing leaf
    and fine root-hairs; standing still through wind
    and rain; their dance is in the flowing spiral grain
        in our minds so be it.

Gratitude to Air, bearing the soaring Swift and the silent
    Owl at dawn. Breath of our song
    clear spirit breeze
        in our minds so be it.

Gratitude to Wild Beings, our brothers, teaching secrets,
    freedoms, and ways; who share with us their milk;
    self-complete, brave, and aware
        in our minds so be it.

Gratitude to Water: clouds, lakes, rivers, glaciers;
    holding or releasing; streaming through all
    our bodies salty seas
        in our minds so be it.

Gratitude to the Sun: blinding pulsing light through
    trunks of trees, through mists, warming caves where
    bears and snakes sleep—he who wakes us—
        in our minds so be it.

Gratitude to the Great Sky
    who holds billions of stars—and goes yet beyond that—
    beyond all powers, and thoughts
    and yet is within us—
    Grandfather Space.
    The Mind is his Wife.

        so be it.

—Gary Snyder, after a Mohawk prayer

EARTH

Made from the Soil

The poetry of earth is never dead.

—John Keats, "On the Grasshopper and Cricket"

e a r t h

PAGE 74

Lichen and moss eat away at the rock, breaking it down into the medium for more life.

OPPOSITE PAGE

Farmers in Peru are framed in the element that created their culture.

ACROSS a bare, rocky landscape, an escarpment crumbles into the valley. It looks barren and lifeless—until we see in the distance a patch of green. This is the fertile patch that feeds the human family. Soil is the element from which we build our bodies and our cultures.

For ten thousand years, human survival has been rooted in this precious raw material of life. Tools and methods have been developed over many generations to maintain and protect the soil; seeds have been selected for their ability to thrive in local conditions. The seasons of the soil govern the entire life of the people who work it— food, festivals, the calendar of ritual, work, and play. The old enemy they work to keep at arm's length is hunger.

Soil is a creation of place, like the crops it produces and the cultures that have grown up around it. Everything grows from the ground up, and the ground is a mixture of everything: animal, vegetable, and mineral. It is an old partnership between the inorganic and the organic, a collaboration between the planet and the life it shelters, an incredible gathering of life.

Weathered by water and wind, broken down by air, water, or life, rock is where soil begins. Life transforms that crumbled rock into the medium for creating more life. In the rubble carved from a mountain by a glacier, you can see that primordial process still under way. On the rock face, the stain of lichen spreads, leaching the rock for useful elements. Invisible bacteria are at work as well, dissolving and concentrating substances they need, reducing mountains to rubble over immense periods of time. Plants, rooting wherever they can find a crevice, grow in the graveyard of their ancestors—the organic remains of uncountable generations of bacteria and plants.

We can only see the beauty that the soil produces. But think for a moment about the hidden world under our feet. It is the kingdom of Hades, the dark world where life is made from death, the region of transformation and rebirth. It is beneath our notice, and yet it is rich beyond imagining. Roots and fibres bind the dark clumps; water drips, pools, and flows; everywhere life swarms. Microscopic grazing creatures are stalked by microscopic predators, while other creatures feed on the waste of both. All the elements—earth and air, energy and water—are at play here, because the earth is like Earth, the microcosm like the macrocosm, made out of the same materials, held together by the same principles, maintained by and maintaining an extraordinary diversity of life.

Landsat images show the limits of Earth's fertility. Seventy-one per cent of the surface is covered with ocean; if you consider the area that is frozen solid, covered by desert, mountains, or fresh water, or paved over—and add in the climate—you can see how little

OPPOSITE PAGE

Terraces form fertile waves on the slopes of Mount Ungaran in
central Java: steps towards a life.

PAGE 80

Rice and beans in a Nepalese market show the diversity that is
crucial to life.

arable land there is. Yet it feeds us all. Ninety per cent of
all humans on Earth live on grain: we're herbivores, grazing on the plant growth of the soil. A small minority of
us put that plant growth through the digestive systems of
other animals before we eat it. But one way or another,
almost all six billion of us depend on that thin brown
layer. Like all terrestrial animals, we're made of it, taking
it in transformed into food, adding to it as organic waste.

Our part in the partnership began about ten thousand years ago. It was a kind of recapitulation of the evolution of life. Just as the arrival of the plants, with their
ability to store sunlight, allowed life to diversify, so the
development of agriculture gave us access to the energy
stored in the soil and allowed us to store it as food and
create reserves. Domesticating plants, animals, and the
soil meant we could diversify—working at more than
just hunting and gathering, creating culture through
agriculture—and we could increase our numbers.

One of the richest of these early agricultural civi-
lizations developed in the fertile alluvial soils of the
Nile Valley. For at least six thousand years, the cycle of
growth, death, and rebirth orchestrated by the annual
flooding of the mighty Nile has included human beings.
Tools and crops depicted on the tombs of the Pharaohs
can be found in the fields on the banks of the Nile
today; wheat originated in this part of the world, and

many of the ancestral varieties developed here long ago
are still planted.

Farmers in many parts of the world still select their
next-year's seed the way their distant ancestors did: by
walking their fields at harvest time and picking out especially vigorous and productive plants. A farmer knows
which field is dry in spring, which is windy, where disease or insects threaten. His seeds are matched over generations to the place they grow; plants self-select by
surviving or doing well there, then the farmer selects
them. Because they are naturally genetically diverse, his
crops can adapt to changing conditions. These techniques created the food crops that feed the world:
resilient, locally adapted, resistant to disease and insects.

Modern agriculture has taken a different approach.
In the past century, more people have been born on
Earth than in all the millennia before. More and more
we are divorced from the soil, living together in cities,
separated from the cycle of fertility by the mechanical,
industrial, and chemical agriculture that produces our
food. We use hybrid seeds in the high-tech, high-yield
farming developed during the late twentieth century.
Engineered for high yields, they are genetically uniform,
designed to take up water and fertilizer in large amounts
to produce a giant harvest. Without the resilience diversity bestows, they need chemical defences against disease

earth

and insect predators and against competition from weeds. And beneath them the soil suffers—the fertilizer feeds the crops but not the soil. The costs to humans and the ecosystem are enormous: the loss of diversity in food crops, the possibility of massive crop failure, the cost of the fossil fuels used, and the deadly destruction of the soil. In the developed world, food travels thousands of kilometres to reach our tables; our appetites are changing world agriculture.

Right now this situation is changing rapidly. Across the industrialized world, farmers are becoming concerned about the costs of chemical agriculture to themselves, their families, and their land. In the cities food shoppers are alert to the risks of chemical residues, of livestock diseases, and of genetically manipulated food crops. They are no longer confident of the safety of their food. New ways, which are often old ways revisited, are being developed to restore the cycle of fertility. Organic agriculture is the fastest-growing agricultural sector in North America. More and more of us are starting to remember where we humans come from and where we're going—back into the living soil.

Behold this compost! behold it well!
Perhaps every mite has once form'd part of a sick person—
Yet behold!
The grass of spring covers the prairies,
The bean bursts noislessly through the mould in the garden,
The delicate spear of the onion pierces upward,
The apple-buds cluster together on the apple-branches,
The resurrection of the wheat appears with pale visage out
of its graves,
The tinge awakes over the willow-tree and the mulberry-tree,
The he-birds carol mornings and evenings, while the she-birds sit
on their nests,
The young of poultry break through the hatch'd eggs,
The new-born of animals appear—the calf is dropt from the cow,
the colt from the mare,
Out of its little hill faithfully rise the potato's dark green leaves,
Out of its hill rises the yellow maize-stalk—the lilacs bloom in
the door-yards;
The summer growth is innocent and disdainful above all those
strata of sour dead.
What chemistry!

—Walt Whitman, *Leaves of Grass*

e a r t h

Dakota children understand that we are of the soil and the soil of us, that we love the birds and beasts that grew with us on this soil. A bond exists between all things because they all drink the same water and breathe the same air.

—Luther Standing Bear, *My People the Sioux*

Farmers in Bali believe that working with the sources of life is the province of the gods. At shrines in their fields like this one, they make offerings to the rice goddess, who sends them the harvest.

With the sweat of thy brow shalt thou eat bread till thou return to earth, for out of it wast thou taken,

for soil thou art and unto soil thou shalt return.

—Genesis 3:19

LEFT

A plant sprouting through a dead cormorant's wing turns death into life.

OPPOSITE PAGE

Death has been dishonoured in this ancient South American graveyard, probably by modern-day vandals. It reminds us of what the rituals of death are for: they celebrate the cycle we are all moving through.

e a r t h

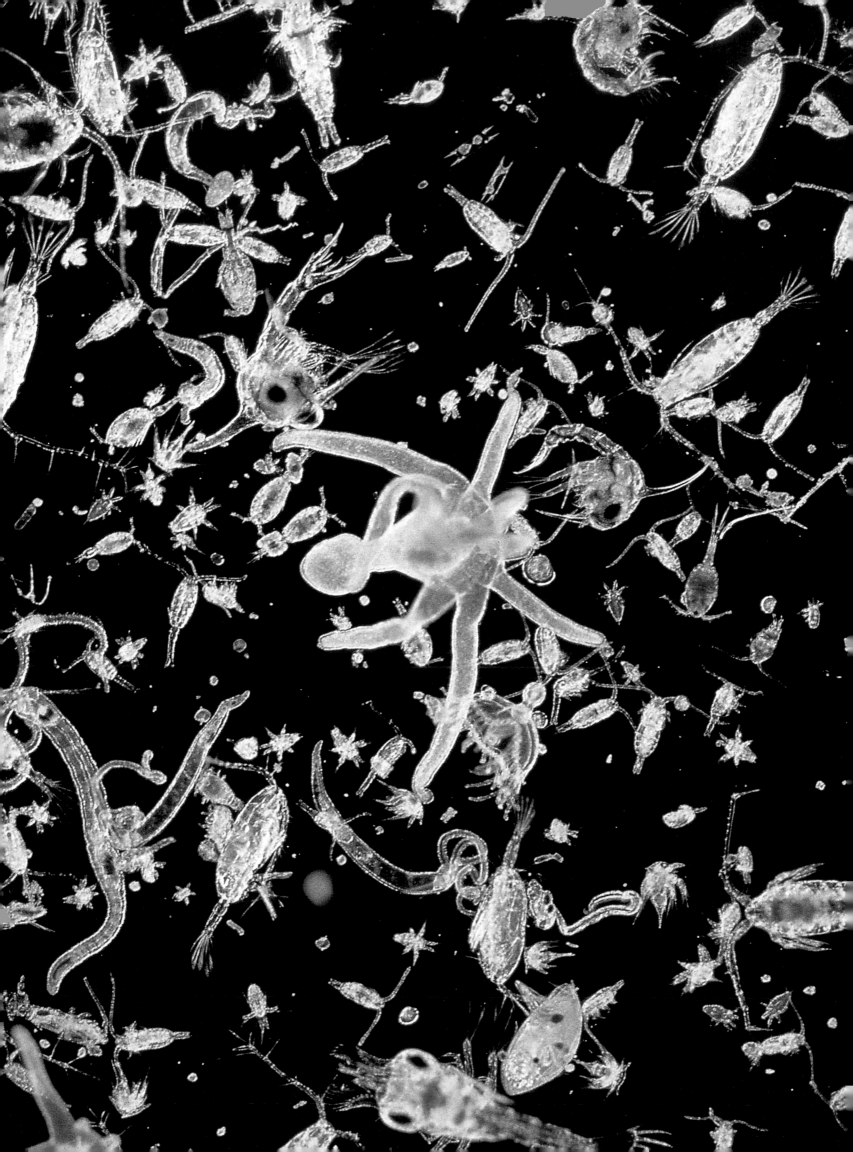

BIODIVERSITY

Protected by Our Kin

The Sixt, and of Creation last arose

With Eevning Harps and Mattin, when God said,

Let th' Earth bring forth Fowle living in her kinde,

Cattel and Creeping things, and Beast of the Earth,

Each in their kinde. The Earth obey'd, and strait

Op'ning her fertile Woomb teem'd at a Birth

Innumerous living Creatures, perfet formes,

Limb'd and full grown . . .

—John Milton, *Paradise Lost,* Book 7

biodiversity

PAGE 86

Marine organisms display the extraordinary diversity present at every level of life.

OPPOSITE PAGE

Golden orb weaver, one of the world's great makers.

WE live in a world built by technology; we're surrounded by the triumphs of our own ingenuity. At least that is how it seems. But everything we need for life comes from nature, and we are completely dependent on Earth's other life forms for our survival. Those sacred elements that together create the conditions necessary for survival are themselves renewed and maintained by the interaction of a vast multitude of different kinds of organisms.

Diversity seems to be the key to this interactive process—the ability of life to adapt to change, to seize opportunities, to recreate itself. Since the very beginning, this process has woven a web of interdependent organisms: as each species finds a way to make a living, it provides opportunities for other species, all existing in multiple sets of interlinked relationships.

Everywhere you look, and everywhere you cannot look, life survives by means of these relationships—this world is designed by the interconnectedness of species from the very largest to the microscopically unimaginable. Organisms that put stuff together, as plants do through photo-synthesis, depend on organisms that take stuff apart, such as the detrivores, which break down organic material, creating more soil for plants to grow in. Both depend on bacteria and fungi, which move nutrients about for other forms of life to utilize. The decom-posers' food supplies are enriched by herbivores and car-nivores, which depend ultimately on the plants' produc-tivity—and so the circle turns. We are dancing in this circle too, fitted in a million different ways into the buzzing, humming, roaring activities of life on Earth. Biodiversity is the name that has been given to the sum total of that life, that crucial element in the sacred bal-ance of the planet.

Diversity is central for each species as well as for the biosphere as a whole. Since the 1960s geneticists have understood that genetic variety in the gene pool of a species is crucial to a species' survival—it is the means by which it is able to adapt. "Silent genes" express them-selves in response to environmental triggers, allowing a species to adapt to this planet's constantly changing con-ditions. In this way a species is made by the place it inhabits. Just as life forms actively shape the conditions for life on Earth, so the planet shapes the organisms that it shelters.

Although we depend on the planet's biodiversity, we know almost nothing about it. We don't even know how many species exist. We do know, however, that of all the known animals, the most numerous by far are insects. It is estimated that there are 200 million insects for every human being on Earth. Insects are the most diverse and successful animals on the planet. They control other

I find among the poems of Schiller

No mention of the caterpillar,

Nor can I find one anywhere

In Petrarch or in Baudelaire,

So here I sit in extra session

To give my personal impression.

The caterpillar, as it's called,

Is often hairy, seldom bald;

It looks as if it never shaves;

When as it walks, it walks in waves;

And from the cradle to the chrysalis

It's utterly speechless, songless, whistleless.

—Ogden Nash, "The Caterpillar"

ABOVE

Three hundred thousand species of beetle have been identified—
one-fifth of all known forms of life. Not many of them wear
coats like this one, a kind of scarab found in the Kalahari.
The "fur" allows it to keep active at night.

biodiversity

insects through predation; they pollinate plants and feed fish, birds, and mammals. Harvard ecologist E. O. Wilson points out that if all humanity went extinct overnight, perhaps half a dozen or so species of bacteria and parasites that can only live on human hosts would also disappear, but the vast majority of life forms would rebound and flourish. In contrast, if all the ants were to vanish overnight, whole ecosystems would collapse, vast numbers of species would go extinct, and major changes in the makeup of life on Earth would ensue.

A few years ago, Terry Erwin of the Smithsonian Institute went to the Amazon rain forest in Peru. He covered an area of forest floor with plastic and delivered a fog of pesticide into the canopy, whereupon a shower of insects fell onto the sheets. Erwin found that virtually every insect he recovered was altogether new to science. On the basis of his findings, he estimated there are over 30 million species of life on Earth. A general consensus seems to be developing that a reasonable number is around 10 million.

To date, Wilson calculates that between 1.4 and 1.6 million species have been recovered and identified—perhaps 15 per cent of the number on Earth. That may simply mean that someone has given a name to a dead plant or animal, not that scientists know anything about the way the species lives or interacts with other forms of life. How

have we acquired such dominance on the planet when we have so little ability to mitigate our deleterious impact?

We have believed ourselves to be masters here, but the problems gathering in air and water, in forests and farmland, and in our hearts and minds are compelling evidence of the limits to our understanding. After a century of overwhelming confidence, we find ourselves uncertain what to do, how to fix things. The problem is, we're searching for answers in the wrong place, looking for technical solutions when what we really need is a whole new way of looking at our world and ourselves. We need to rediscover our species' ancient understanding of our kinship with all creation so that instead of waging war on the natural world, we can find our place in it.

A parliament of Atlantic puffins in Iceland.

The sloth is not alone. A species of moth is adapted to live in the
fur of the three-toed sloth and only there.

Street scene in India. Cultural diversity is what counts for us
humans. Every culture represents a different possibility.

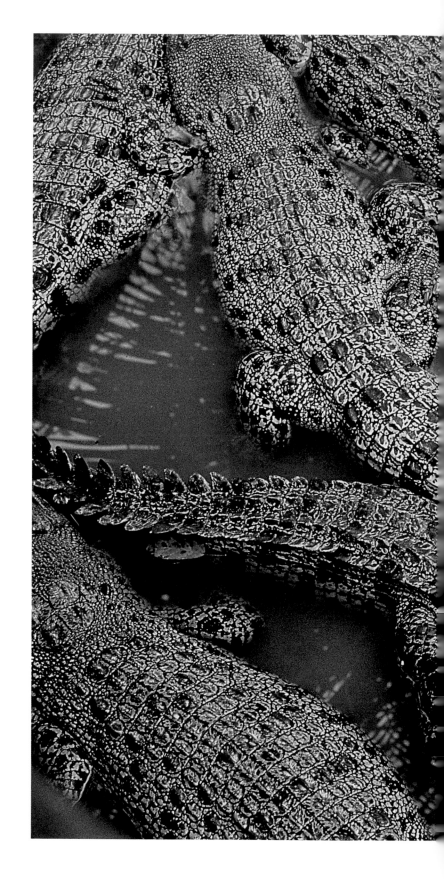

PAGES 96–97

Zebras and gnus find common space on the grasslands of Kenya.

RIGHT

Crocodiles in Borneo show similarity and diversity: patterns vary, yet they stay the same.

b i o d i v e r s i t y

A thing is right when it tends to preserve the integrity,
stability and beauty of the biotic community.
It is wrong when it tends otherwise.

—Aldo Leopold

This alpine meadow on Mount Rainier, Washington, is a
community shaped precisely by and for its place.

The prayer wheel of Nepal
reflects our kinship with all
creation.

b i o d i v e r s i t y

All nature is linked together by invisible bonds, and every organic creature however low,

however feeble, however dependent, is necessary to the well-being of some other

among the myriad forms of life with which the Creator has peopled the Earth.

—George Perkins Marsh, *Man and Nature*

Although human beings display great diversity in their cultures, some things are universal—such as the relationship between grandfather and grandchild.

Life is more than a live green scum on a dead pool,
a shimmering scurf like slime mold on rock. Look at the
planet. Everywhere freedom twines its way around
necessity, inventing new strings of occasion, lassoing time
and putting it through its varied and spirited paces.
Everywhere live things lash at the rocks.

—Annie Dillard, "Life on the Rocks, the Galapagos,"
Teaching a Stone to Talk

Coral reefs are among the planet's most productive ecosystems.
Coral polyps harbour photosynthetic bacteria and build their
underwater cities with the energy of the sun. These reefs are the
largest structures life has made on Earth.

biodiversity

OPPOSITE PAGE

False turkey-tail fungus. There may be 100,000 species of fungi on Earth, or there may be more than a million. No one knows for sure.

ABOVE

The commercial orchid these days is the opposite of biodiverse. Plants are reproduced by cloning and so are genetically identical.

FOLLOWING PAGES

This katydid collection from Costa Rica shows an astonishing range of camouflage—one reason for biodiversity.

LOVE

The Tie That Binds

Love, from whom the world begun,

Hath the secret of the sun.

Love can tell, and love alone,

Whence the million stars were strewn,

Why each atom knows its own.

—Robert Bridges, "9," *New Poems*

love

love

PAGE 110

Child and mother are tied together in a web of chemicals, emotions, and sensations.

OPPOSITE PAGE

Humans are intensely social animals.

CHILDREN run to grab their father's leg, their friends, their pet dog, their hamster. Teenagers gaze into each other's eyes, movie stars kiss while fireworks burst behind them, bed sheets toss and flap while couples couple, old folk hold hands and eat another sandwich. Achilles mourns Patroclus in his tent, Romeo calls out to Juliet in the orchard, Falstaff and Mistress Quickly share a bawdy joke. Mother Theresa washes the wounds of the homeless, and sons take mothers out to birthday lunches. Dog owners pet their small, fat, bad-tempered pugs, parents lift and cradle infants, pointing out their beauty, brains, and promise.

What is this powerful attraction we call love? From culture to culture, from era to era, however the stories vary, the connection between human beings is always front and centre. In our culture we see love as emotional, sentimental, passionate—a matter of choice, a meeting of souls. What if instead it is built into our cells— or even into the cosmos?

The entanglement that begins in the womb doesn't unravel at birth. Ancient, invisible cords tie mothers and babies together, physically as well as emotionally. They know each other by smell, respond physically to each other's sounds, affect each other's hormones, disturb each other's dreams. We are programmed to love our young. It is just as well; without being loved, it seems, a child cannot love. Without that crucial reciprocal relationship, the child may not even survive.

In 1989, when the Romanian dictator Nicolae Ceausescu was executed, a grim experiment on child development was revealed. Between 100,000 and 300,000 children were in institutions; most had received no more than subsistence levels of care and minimal contact with adults. Studies of these children over the past decade, thousands of whom were adopted by North Americans, have charted the consequences. Many were physically stunted, slow in speech development, prone to attention deficits and temper tantrums, and hypersensitive to touch. MRI scans showed abnormal brain development. Other research confirms these findings: lack of love and nurturing affects the totality of human development. But there is another side to this story. Since being adopted into a loving family, many of these children have experienced the extraordinary power of love to heal.

Human beings are intensely social animals; we depend on each other throughout life. Each group develops a culture that encodes the rules for living with each other and with the surrounding world. Each culture is a complex continuing record of the group's history and experience, woven from lessons learned over time. That record is localized: it describes how to live *here*, in this particular environment. We gain our sense of place from

It was Eros who plaited garlands of fruit and flowers, / Who poured dense gold from a pitcher into sunrises and sunsets. / He and no one else led us into fragrant landscapes / Of branches hanging low by streams, of gentle hills, / And an echo lured us on and on, a cuckoo promised / A place, deep in a thicket, where there is no longing

—Czeslaw Milosz, "Diary of a Naturalist"

each other, from our shared past, present, and future: this process teaches us who we are individually and collectively, and it shapes how we present ourselves.

This need for love is not confined to humans, as two zoologists showed in 1962. Baby monkeys taken from their mothers at birth were offered two mother substitutes in their cage. One was made of wire and contained food; the other was made of soft terry cloth but had no food. The babies clung to the soft form, choosing the merest hint of parental nurturing in preference to food. They grew up with a variety of abnormal behaviours, including a lack of interest in raising young. This experimental evidence casts doubt on our characteristic distinction between *love*, which is human, and *instinct*, which we apply to every other living being. Taught to be wary of anthropomorphism, perhaps instead we have been arrogant.

Biologists point to evidence in other species. Baboons develop lifelong friendships and may risk their own lives to help a friend. Adult female elephants hold up sick companions to prevent a fatal fall and cooperate to dig a baby out of a mudhole. A wolf pack is really a family—its members are closely related and mutually supportive. Hunting together, they bring and share food with the family. Wolf expert John Theberge suggests that what looks like baby-sitting is exactly that: while other adults are out hunting, an aunt or a cousin takes care of the pups.

We ourselves are aggregations of trillions of cells. Each cell contains remnants of earlier invasions by bacteria. Integrated into the cells, these microbial relics performed services, respiring in return for protection and nourishment. Each of us is a community of organisms, and each of us belongs to a larger community of organisms aggregated for mutual benefit—the key as always is reciprocity. Biologist Lynn Margulis tells us that all animals and plants were formed by a process of symbiogenesis—by combination, not competition.

Move through the nested circles of your community. The first circle consists of the organelles within your cells. This circle is followed by the aggregation of cells, bacteria, parasites, and symbionts making up your body and then by your family, friends, and neighbours. The next circle contains a larger set of relationships: your crucial, inbuilt need for the company of other forms of life. Molecular biology shows that all living organisms are closely related, confirming the ancient kinship of life on Earth. E. O. Wilson has coined the term *biophilia*, defined as "the innate tendency to focus on life and life-like processes." We are part of a web that includes the entirety of the living world. That is the law of love.

But modern life has torn that web by massively increasing the size of human aggregations. Already more than half the world's people live in cities, and urban growth

love

A Persian love scene from
the seventeenth century.
In a multitude of forms,
attraction holds the universe
together.

Toulouse-Lautrec's painting of a couple entitled *The Bed*: comfort, trust, repose between two people.

love

is happening fastest in the developing world. Moving house from town to town, surrounded by the anonymity of urban streetscape, we no longer know where we live, so we wonder who we are. In nursing homes, day-care centres, architects' offices, urban parks, shopping centres, zoos, and gardens, we can track the benefits of satisfying the need city dwellers have for contact with nature. It is no accident, Wilson says, that more people visit zoos in North America than attend all major sporting events combined. They are visiting their relatives.

Philosophers and writers as diverse as Erasmus, Ghandi, and Thomas Berry argue this idea further. In different ways they claim that love is the key to the universe, the desire for union that draws atoms together, the tug of any body with mass at any other body with mass. Cosmologist Brian Swimme asserts that in the movements of the solar system—planets circling the central star, satellites circling the planets—we see the reciprocal allurement that binds the cosmos. As well as emotion, sentiment, passion, is love the way we humans experience the nature of all creation?

Sociability is as much a law of nature as mutual struggle. If we ask nature: "Who are the fittest: those who are continually at war with each other, or those who support one another?" we at once see that those animals which acquire habits of mutual aid are undoubtedly the finest.

—Peter Kropotkin, *Mutual Aid*

love

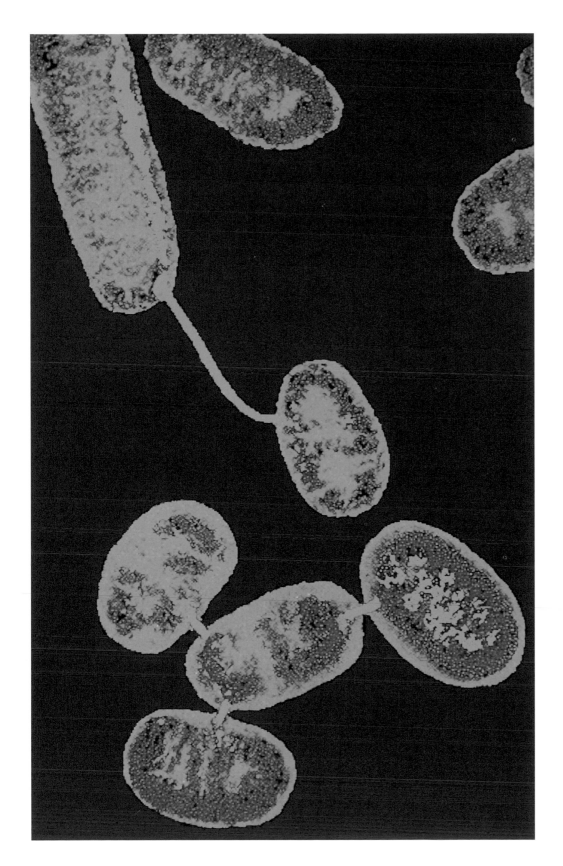

The Arnolfini Wedding by Jan
van Eyck shows us one way
of mating.

LEFT
Describing behaviour as
"loving" may be harder to
accept when the organisms
are less like us. Take a look
at the basic forms of life:
attraction between E.coli cell
membranes draws them
together, and the bacteria
fuse in the act of genetic
recombination, like flora and
fauna with sexual cycles.

ABOVE

Rock art from Vermont shows the sheep version of the
all-important family.

OPPOSITE PAGE

A mother and her child know each other by taste, by smell, by
sound, by feel.

love

love

OPPOSITE PAGE

Love breeds love in a perpetual process of exchange.

ABOVE

The deep connection between people defeats time and space.

It transcends life and death.

Like human beings, polar bears and their young are intensely interconnected through all the early stages of life.

In a Berber village, Morocco, the web of loving attention binds the group.

love

We and the beasts are kin, Man has nothing that the animals have not at least a vestige of; the animals have nothing that man in some degree does not share. Since, then, the animals are creatures with wants and feelings, differing in degree only from our own, they surely have their rights.

—Ernest Thompson Seton

Like young humans, young elephants need a long period of care from their parents.

love

Love is above the laws, above the opinion of men;
it is the truth, the flame, the pure element,
the primary idea of the moral world.

—Madame de Staël, *Zulma and other Tales*

From birth to death, we need each other to survive.

love

SPIRIT

Sacred Matter

And I have felt

A presence that disturbs me with the joy

Of elevated thoughts; a sense sublime

Of something far more deeply interfused,

Whose dwelling is the light of setting suns,

And the round ocean and the living air,

And the blue sky, and in the mind of man:

A motion and a spirit, that impels

All thinking things, all objects of all thought,

And rolls through all things.

—William Wordsworth, "Lines Composed a Few Miles above Tintern Abbey"

spirit

spirit

PAGE 130

Barranquilla's Carnival, Colombia. We put on the supernatural, enacting our connection to the world beyond the everyday.

OPPOSITE PAGE

We may imagine we're in charge, but a single wave can quickly disillusion us.

HUMANS see beyond the moment—remembering the past, anticipating the future, continuously trying to make sense of our experience. We construct a world, and it has forces in it, powers beyond ours. As far as we know, as far as our stories tell us, we have always believed that there are holy places on Earth, which are the dwelling places of the spirits, the sources of life. Our stories tell us what is sacred in our world—the central elements of survival, the necessities on which life's continuity depends. They present the world as we conceive it, the story of our place and purpose—where we come from, what we're made of, where we're going.

The sacred rivers of the Hindu pantheon, the primacy of the sun in most polytheistic cultures, the Earth goddesses, the animal spirits that have been the gods and guides of many hunting peoples—these are just a few of the countless ways we have pieced together and expressed the way things work on Earth. Earth is alive and powerful, the gods inhabit the world, and we are part of it, dependent, astonished, and respectful. There must be the appropriate rituals: the casting of the salt, the offering to Pachamama, the singing of the songline. Spirit is beyond science. It is our way of acknowledging our place on Earth.

For most of our time on Earth we have been small, tasty, unarmoured animals, prey to every large carnivore looking for a meal. Over time we developed a powerful defence—our pattern-making, restless, enormous, ingenious brains. Since then, our consciousness has marked us out. Like a few other primates, and perhaps some marine mammals, we are *self*-conscious, recognizing ourselves as individuals, learning about the powers and limits of our separate selves. Consciousness divides us from each other and the world; it also gives us the means by which we can transcend that division. We can learn from experience and teach others what we have learned. We can imagine another's existence and respond to it. We can reconstruct the world as we see it and reenact our connection with it.

Consciousness warns us that just as we had a beginning, so we must come to an end. Longing to transcend mortality, from our earliest days we have built burial places where we surround our dead with food and drink, paintings, or possessions to ease their journey onwards. We have designed and decorated sacred places, mounds and barrows, pyramids and caves, mausoleums, memorials, and cities of the dead—structures that outlast generations, carrying the stories into the future, asserting the endless primacy of life.

In Australia, rock paintings tens of thousands of years old belong to a culture that still persists. Ask the Aborigines, and you might hear from them that these sacred places connect directly to the Dreamtime, the

OPPOSITE PAGE

Buddhists imagine a world held together by spirit, in which form appears out of nothingness and returns to it.

everlasting and continuous process of creation. *All* life is the *same* life, shaped by and for the place it lives; the same fertility rituals that pray for plentiful game animals are used to prepare women for motherhood. *All* life is the *same* life, moving through time and space and through a million forms. Mortality is a transition continually experienced by matter on Earth, which is never lost, but always altering and changing in a constant process of transformation.

Ours is the first society to separate the sacred from knowledge and power, to sequester it as "religion"— steeped in rewards and punishments but cut off from the material world and the technology with which we manipulate it. Science has given us the executive power, by exorcising the spirits, the powers that make the patterns. We have been pulled apart into sections, made into minds that operate on our own bodies, on each other, on the world around us. This system of accumulating knowledge has built an extraordinary world, but it excludes the element we need to thrive—the wholeness and connection that we call spirit.

Art also has been relegated to the sidelines, though it has always been one of the central ways in which human beings express their relationship to the whole, their vision of the world they inhabit. The more intense our emphasis becomes on the individual, the more we sequester the divine from the material, the eternal from the dailiness of life, the less we are aware of the elements that move into, through, and beyond us. As we lose the rituals of respect, we lose our sense of the sacred—our understanding of our part in it.

Life itself is the sacred on Earth, living in balance with the planet that created it. We've constructed a misleading opposition between matter and spirit. But spirit is not somewhere else, something else; it is the whole interwoven connectivity of life. Just as in love we may glimpse the force that holds the universe together, our longing for spirituality draws us back to where we belong. It may be our chiefest survival mechanism, leading us to value and respect the precious elements of life.

We know what and who we are: made from water and air, fire and earth, the elements that make up all creation, part of the interconnected, interdependent web of life, woven with all other living things into a reciprocal relationship with the planet. We have never left Eden, that infinitely complex and beautiful world that gave us birth, shaped our minds and bodies, and sustains us every moment of life. We are born into its endless aggregation and disaggregation of matter. We need to rediscover and celebrate our place here; there is nowhere else for us to live.

spirit

Many of the world's religions
hold the same four elements
sacred: earth, air, fire, and
water. Hinduism, the
religion of India, adds
a fifth: spirit.

spirit

s p i r i t

Heaven and earth, the watered plains, the moon's shining globe, the sun and stars are all strengthened by Spirit working

within them, and mind stirs this great mass, infused through all its limbs and mixed in with its body.

—Virgil, *Aeneid* VI.724–727

All cultures acknowledge powers beyond our powers and have
rituals with which to honour them.

spirit

spirit

Soul clap its hands and sing, and louder sing

For every tatter in its mortal dress

—W. B. Yeats, "Sailing to Byzantium"

Gathering together, reading the sacred text, observing the protocols—these are the ways humans enact the presence of spirit. Here Muslim women read from the Koran.

RIGHT

A sumo wrestler casts a ritual offering of salt before the match begins.

OPPOSITE PAGE

Nis'ga totem echoes the powers of forest, mountain, and sky.

spirit

Man has been driven out of the paradise in which

he could trust his instincts.

—Konrad Lorenz

The Wedded Rocks represents the eternal union of Izanami and
Izanagi, two Japanese Shinto deities who gave birth to the islands
of the Japanese archipelago.

Do you think you can take the world and improve it? / I do not think it can be done. /
The world is sacred. / You cannot improve it. If you try to change it, you will ruin it. /
If you try to help it, you will lose it.

—Lao Tzu

OPPOSITE PAGE

On the Day of the Dead, many cultures reconnect with the ones that have gone before.

ABOVE

In Angkor Wat a fig tree transfigures a temple.

PAGES 146—47

We have never left Eden. Earth is alive and we are part of its sacred balance.

NOTES

INTRODUCTION

p. 1, par. 1. Wade Davis, *Light at the Edge of the World* (Vancouver: Douglas & McIntyre, 2002).

p. 1, par. 3. Peter Knudtson and David T. Suzuki, *Wisdom of the Elders* (Toronto: Stoddart, 1992).

p. 1, par. 4. Roger Penrose, *The Emperor's New Mind* (New York: Vintage, 1989). Also "Quantum non-locality and complex reality" in *The Simulation of Human Intelligence*, edited by D. Broadbent (Cambridge: Blackwell, 1993).

p. 1, par. 4. Brian Swimme, *The Universe is a Green Dragon* (Santa Fe: Bear & Company, 1984).

p. 2, par. 1. Brian Swimme. Personal communication on all data about the Sun.

p. 2, par. 4. James Lovelock, *Gaia: A New Look at Life on Earth* (New York: Oxford University Press, 1979).

p. 2, par. 5. Gary Taubes, "Why Water Is Weird," *Red Herring*, March 20, 2001.

p. 3, par. 3. Stephen J. Pyne, *World Fire: The Culture of Fire on Earth* (New York: Holt, 1995).

p. 3, par. 3. Lynn Margulis, *Symbiosis in Cell Evolution* (San Francisco: W. H. Freeman & Company, 1981).

p. 5. Alejandro Lerner, quoted in *Save the Earth* by Jonathan Porritt (London: Dorling Kindersley Ltd., 1991).

p. 6, par. 2. Stephen Jay Gould, *Wonderful Life: The Burgess Shale and the Nature of History* (New York: W. W. Norton & Company, 1989).

p. 6, par. 2. James K. Fredrickson and Tullis Onstott, "Microbes Deep Inside the Earth," *Scientific American* 275 (October 1996):68.

p. 8, par. 3. *Science* 291, no. 5507 (February 16, 2001). Entire issue is devoted to the human genome and its significance.

p. 8, par. 3. Edward O. Wilson, *Biophilia: The Human Bond with Other Species* (Cambridge, Mass.: Harvard University Press, 1984).

p. 17, par. 3. David T. Suzuki, "Temperature-sensitive mutations in *Drosophila melanogaster*," *Science* 170:695, 1970.

p. 18, par. 1. Rachel Carson, *Silent Spring* (Boston: Houghton Mifflin, 1962).

p. 18. Prince Sadruddin Aga Khan, quoted in *Save the Earth* by Jonathan Porritt (London: Dorling Kindersley Ltd., 1991).

p. 22, par. 3. David Suzuki, *The Sacred Balance* (Vancouver: David Suzuki Foundation/Greystone Books, 1997).

p. 24, par. 3. Ashley Montagu, *The Direction of Human Development* (New York: Harper, 1955).

p. 24, par. 3. D. E. Johnson *et al.*, "The health of children adopted in Romania," *Journal of the American Medical Association* 268 (December 23, 1992):3446.

p. 23. Yoko Ono, *Earth Piece (Summer 1990)*, quoted in *Save the Earth* by Jonathan Porritt (London: Dorling Kindersley Ltd., 1991).

p. 27, par. 1. Bill McKibben, *The End of Nature* (New York: Random House, 1989).

WATER

p. 29. Philip Larkin, "Water" from *Collected Poems* (New York: Farrar, Straus, & Giroux, 1989).

p. 40. Thor Heyerdahl, *The Ra Expeditions* (Garden City, N.Y.: Doubleday, 1971).

p. 43. Samuel Taylor Coleridge, *Kubla Khan*, in *The Norton Anthology of English Literature* (New York: W.W. Norton, 1987).

AIR

p. 47. William Wordsworth, "The Prelude," in *The Norton Anthology of English Literature* (New York: W.W. Norton, 2000).

p. 51. William Shakespeare, *Hamlet* (New York: Dover Publications, 1992).

p. 52. Gerard Manley Hopkins, "The Blessed Virgin compared to the Air we Breathe," from *The Poetry of Gerard Manley Hopkins*, edited by W. H. Gardner and N. H. Mackenzie (Oxford: Oxford University Press, 1967).

p. 56. Vladimir Shatalov, quoted in *The Home Planet*, edited by Kevin W. Kelley (Herts, U.K.: Queen Anne Press, 1988).

FIRE

p. 61. Walt Whitman, "Song of Myself," *Leaves of Grass* (Oxford: Oxford University Press, 1990).

p. 65. Johann Wolfgang von Goethe, *Goethe's Werke, I* (Hamburg: Christian Wegner Verlag, 1948).

p. 69, **par.** 1. Stephen J. Pyne, *World Fire: The Culture of Fire on Earth* (New York: Holt, 1995).

p. 72. Gary Snyder, "Prayer for the Great Family," from *Turtle Island* (New York: New Directions, 1974).

EARTH

p. 75. John Keats, "On the Grasshopper and Cricket" in *The Complete Poems of John Keats* (New York: Modern Library, 1994).

p. 81. Walt Whitman, *Leaves of Grass* (Oxford: Oxford University Press, 1990).

p. 83. Luther Standing Bear, *My People the Sioux* (Boston: Houghton Mifflin, 1928).

BIODIVERSITY

p. 87. John Milton, *Paradise Lost*, from *The Riverside Milton*, edited by Roy Flanagan (Boston: Houghton Mifflin: 1998).

p. 90. Ogden Nash, "The Caterpillar," from *I Wouldn't Have Missed It: Selected Poems of Ogden Nash* (Boston: Little, Brown, 1975).

p. 101. Aldo Leopold, quoted in *The Way: An Ecological World-View* by Edward Goldsmith (Athens: University of Georgia Press, 1998).

p. 103. George Perkins Marsh, *Man and Nature* (Cambridge, Mass.: Belknap Press, 1965).

p. 105. Annie Dillard, "Life on the Rocks, the Galapagos," from *Teaching a Stone to Talk* (New York: Harper & Row, 1982).

LOVE

p. 111. Robert Bridges, "9," *Poetical Works, Excluding the Eight Dramas & the Testament of Beauty* (Oxford: Oxford University Press, 1947).

p. 114. Czeslaw Milosz, "Diary of a Naturalist," *Bells in Winter* (New York: Ecco Press, 1996).

p. 117. Peter Kropotkin, *Mutual Aid: A Factor in Evolution* (Montreal: Black Rose Books, 1989).

p. 126. Ernest Thompson Seton, quoted in *The Way: An Ecological World-View* by Edward Goldsmith (Athens: University of Georgia Press, 1998).

p. 128. Madame de Staël, from *An Extraordinary Woman: Selected Writings of Germaine de Staël* (New York: Columbia University Press, 1987).

SPIRIT

p. 131. William Wordswoth, "Lines Composed a Few Miles above Tintern Abbey on Revisiting the Wye during a Tour," from *The Norton Anthology of English Literature* (New York: W.W. Norton, 1987).

p. 137. Virgil, *Aeneid* vi. 724–727 (New York: P. F. Collier, 1909).

p. 139. W. B. Yeats, "Sailing to Byzantium," from *The Tower* (New York: Macmillan & Co., 1928).

p. 143. Konrad Lorenz, quoted in *The Way: An Ecological World-View* by Edward Goldsmith (Athens: University of Georgia Press, 1998).

p. 145. Lao Tzu, quoted in *The Way: An Ecological World-View* by Edward Goldsmith (Athens: University of Georgia Press, 1998).

PHOTO CREDITS